THE FALL AND RISE OF
LEYTON ORIENT

THE FALL AND RISE OF
LEYTON ORIENT

The Fairytale Revival of One of Football's Oldest Clubs

SIMON COOPER

First published by Pitch Publishing, 2024

Pitch Publishing
9 Donnington Park,
85 Birdham Road,
Chichester, West Sussex,
PO20 7AJ
www.pitchpublishing.co.uk
info@pitchpublishing.co.uk

© 2024, Simon Cooper

Every effort has been made to trace the copyright.
Any oversight will be rectified in future editions at the
earliest opportunity by the publisher.

All rights reserved. No part of this book may be reproduced,
sold or utilised in any form or transmitted in any form or by
any means, electronic or mechanical, including photocopying,
recording or by any information storage and retrieval system,
without prior permission in writing from the Publisher.

A CIP catalogue record is available for this book
from the British Library.

ISBN 978 1 80150 686 1

Printed and bound in the UK on FSC® certified paper in line
with our continuing commitment to ethical business practices,
sustainability and the environment.

Typesetting and origination by Pitch Publishing
Printed and bound by CPI Anthony Rowe, UK

Contents

Introduction	9
Chapter 1	13
Chapter 2	21
Chapter 3	31
Chapter 4	45
Chapter 5	52
Chapter 6	61
Chapter 7	76
Chapter 8	89
Chapter 9	122
Chapter 10	126
Chapter 11	142
Chapter 12	164
Chapter 13	178
Chapter 14	185
Chapter 15	190
Chapter 16	193
Chapter 17	205
Chapter 18	228
Chapter 19	231
Acknowledgements	238

For Mum, Dad and Ally, you've always been there for me.

For Hannah and Mabel, I'll always be there for you.

Except on Saturday afternoons when Orient are at home.

Introduction

Welcome to Leyton

Saturday, 22 April 2023
BBC Radio 4, *News at 10pm*
'The world of entertainment is paying tribute to Barry Humphries who has died at the age of 89 ... British nationals trapped by the fighting in Sudan say they feel forgotten by the UK government. Also tonight, after 15 years of hurt, ecstasy for Wrexham AFC and the club's Hollywood owners.'

Forget Wrexham for a minute. This story starts in London.

There's a theory about Cockneys; they're not where they're supposed to be. Most of them are in the sticks. The children and grandchildren of the roll-out-the-barrel, two-fingers-to-Hitler Cockneys all moved out of town years ago. It's all stories of a knees-up with Chas and Dave down the Birdcage or 'my nan knew the older Kray twin', but most of the families telling these tales don't live in the East End. They haven't for years. Some stayed, yes, some moved back, but most left London over the past half-century, rolling out to the country, following the trunk roads to Loughton, Brentwood, Cheshunt and Broxbourne, taking their accents and their stories and settling in the greener spaces of the new East End of Essex and East Herts.

A working-class tribe, now often a middle-class tribe with working-class pretensions, they took their football teams with them. And each week they return home. To Arsenal, Tottenham and West Ham, a few to Brisbane Road and Leyton Orient. Back to the same pubs, to the old grounds or the new stadiums, with the same walks from the tube, the same pie at half-time. Sticking to the same places because that's the London they know. The only things that haven't changed. Like birds heading south, coming together in the same places they have for decades. Dads and lads, at peace. Daughters and girlfriends, wives and mums. Drinking down the optimism and the disappointment in the same old boozers they always have. Back where they belong. Their home where they don't live.

This, like all football, is a love story. A love story about misfits finding a home. Leyton Orient have always been a team that have to fight for attention, trapped between the much-loved giants of West Ham, Tottenham and Arsenal. Never able to compete with the 'Glory, Glory' of Tottenham Hotspur, the 'Invincibles' and old money of Arsenal or the mythical 'West Ham Way'. Little Leyton Orient are the forgotten London club.

When Richie Wellens led them to the League Two title in 2023, nobody cared. It was all about Ryan Reynolds, Rob McElhenney and Wrexham. On BBC Radio 5 Live, the soundtrack to the nation's football on a Saturday afternoon, they squeezed in some trailers during the half-time commentary of an FA Cup semi-final, 'For Wrexham in the National League it is now simple. Beat Boreham Wood; get promoted, today. We'll also be reflecting on Rochdale's relegation from the Football League. Huge congratulations, meanwhile, to Leyton Orient, champions of League Two.'

'Huge congratulations, *meanwhile*.' An afterthought to the main story. At this point, Wrexham hadn't even kicked

INTRODUCTION

off in their title-deciding match to win the National League, the league below Leyton Orient, but it was still the most important story of the sporting day. A week later, Rob McElhenney would try and persuade former Welsh captain and genuine footballing superstar Gareth Bale to come out of retirement. It was reported on Radio 4's *Today* programme. Their non-league fairytale was the story everyone was focusing on.

But it's not the only fairytale that played out that day. The fall and rise of Leyton Orient, London's second-oldest professional club, is a story with just as much blockbuster appeal as *Welcome to Wrexham*. There are characters just as big and interesting, playing out stories with twists and turns worthy of any Hollywood script. Full of dramatic triumphs and tragic, heartbreaking lows. A community inspired and reborn. Fuelled by doughnuts and wagon wheels. Misfits coming together from all over the world to be part of a true East End fantasy.

Welcome to Leyton.

And like all stories, there are heroes and villains. This story starts with a saviour, far more hero than villain. A working-class boy from Dagenham, on the outskirts of the East End. A man who started his working life as a chartered accountant because his mum said you never see a poor one and he wouldn't have to worry about money again. A misfit in a world of bowler hats. A man unafraid to do things his way. And a man who, in 1995, bought Leyton Orient for less than a fiver.

1

May 2014. Leyton Orient are on the brink of the Championship, the second tier of English football. Only a play-off final against Rotherham United stands in their way. Win, they go up. Lose, they remain in League One. They haven't been higher than the bottom two divisions in over 30 years.

Barry Hearn has owned the club for 19 years. He's only seen them promoted once in that time.

'It does not get any better than that!'
Sunday, 25 May 2014, Wembley Stadium

Leyton Orient vs Rotherham United, League One play-off final.

'I remember every second of that day,' says Barry Hearn. 'I couldn't have been happier.'

Walking into Wembley was the culmination of nearly two decades of his life.

'I remember arriving with my family. And the excitement running through your veins ... there wouldn't be a need for illegal drugs if you could put that in a bottle and have a mouthful every day.'

It's 3pm as Hearn takes his seat for kick-off. Over 43,000 fans are in the ground alongside the Leyton Orient owner.

The stands are a sea of red reflecting the home kits of both Orient and Rotherham United. Below, the Wembley pitch is half in shadow, half brilliant sunlight; the stadium blocking the mid-afternoon sun from end-to-end down one side of the playing surface. Some players are playing in comparative darkness.

There are two sides to this match.

The occasion is everything Hearn has wanted from owning Leyton Orient, the club he first went to watch as a young boy. 'I saw it as an adventure, like a little child,' he says. 'What kid that goes to watch a football match when he's 11 years old doesn't dream of either playing for that team or owning that team. It's a dream. And I ticked my dream, which I shall forever be grateful for.'

After 33 minutes, Orient win a free kick near the halfway line. Diminutive forward Dean Cox – fan favourite and subject of the chant 'We've got tiny Cox, we've got tiny Cox' – is playing on the left wing. He launches the ball high into the Rotherham penalty area. It's headed clear and lands just outside the box, directly in front of Orient's young winger, Moses Odubajo. Twenty-five yards out, he controls the ball on his chest and strikes it with his left foot, hitting the sweetest half-volley of his life. Rotherham goalkeeper Adam Collin barely moves as the ball flashes past him into the top corner of the net. He simply holds his hands out in disbelief. Odubajo wheels away, ripping his shirt off in celebration.

'It does not get any better than that!' screams Daniel Mann, commentating for Sky Sports.

Four minutes later, it does.

Odubajo is involved again, striking the ball across the Rotherham six-yard box for Cox to tap in at the far post. Orient fans can't believe what they're seeing. Tiny Cox has done it again. The emotion is etched on the fans' faces. Barry Hearn is on his feet, a triumphant fist in the air.

CHAPTER 1

Leading 2-0 in the play-off final at Wembley. And it's not even half-time.

'They couldn't pay their milk bill'

I first meet Barry Hearn at Mascalls, the large country mansion he bought as the Hearn family home. It's now the headquarters of Matchroom Sport, his sports promotion company. Through Matchroom, Hearn built his boxing promotion empire and turned snooker into the TV sensation of the 1980s. As Steve Davis's manager, he transformed the sport, making deals around the world. More recently, Matchroom have led the renaissance of the Professional Darts Corporation, selling out Alexandra Palace every Christmas and turning a pub sport into a multimillion-pound Sky Sports event.

When Hearn bought Leyton Orient for £2.43 in 1995, they were in dire straits. As famously documented in the Channel 4 short film, *Club For A Fiver*, Leyton Orient were about to be relegated with debts of £2m. Over Hearn's two decades in charge, he stabilised the club and took them from the foot of the fourth tier to the brink of the Championship.

'They were losing about half a million quid a year,' he says, remembering the state of the club he took over. 'They couldn't pay their milk bill. Absolutely brassic. No money.'

Owning a football club went against every one of Hearn's business instincts. For once, his heart ruled his head. He describes owning Leyton Orient as 'a pile of aggravation', but he remembers his time in charge with real fondness. Looking back on the run to Wembley in 2014, his eyes light up. He's animated, excited. His manager Russell Slade (the man Hearn describes as 'without a doubt my best appointment') had curated an exciting brand of attacking football.

'Russell Slade takes the credit for me,' says Hearn. 'He lived the job. He was there seven days a week. His family was living up in the north-east. He had a flat in the ground. He was a thorough professional man and a really nice guy. We had something very special in those days.'

Slade (we'll meet him properly later) describes his squad as 'a great group'. A team full of characters. 'I had proper men in the team,' he says. 'It was a small squad, but they all knew their jobs. We all worked hard. I can go back to the first game of that season. Away from home at Carlisle, and we won 5-1. You just felt we could have something that year.'

Hearn tells the story of how he installed a giant map in the dressing room, drawing a line between London and Las Vegas. He added points along the line, with Las Vegas being the target of the 80-something points that would get them in the play-offs. His promise being that if the team got there, he'd take them on a jolly to the States.

The captain, Nathan Clark, was given a special responsibility.

'I gave him a plastic aeroplane,' says Hearn. 'And I divided it between London and Las Vegas. I said, "Every time we get a point, you're the only person who can touch this airplane, and you're going to pull it and pull it." They were more concerned with moving that airplane than win bonuses! They were going, "Clarkey, Clarkey – move us! We got three points! Move us! Where are we now?" "Well, we're just going over Land's End." And it ran the whole season. It was just the most pleasurable season.'

Back to Wembley, and Orient are 2-0 up at half-time. Hearn is enjoying the hospitality when the chairman of Rotherham, Tony Stewart, seeks him out. Hearn describes the exchange of words, 'He said, "Ey up lad. You're far better than us. You deserve this." I said, "Keep your mouth shut, son. There's 45 minutes to go."'

CHAPTER 1

Devastation and desolation

By 60 minutes, it's 2-2. In the 54th minute, Orient goalkeeper Jamie Jones fails to clear a set piece. Former Os striker Alex Revell pounces, stabbing the ball in from close range. 'The battle rages again!' says Daniel Mann in the commentary box.

Five minutes later, Revell scores again. This time it's the goal of his life.

'He scored a wonder goal from like 35 yards,' says Barry Hearn. 'I was directly behind him. I actually saw from the moment he kicked it, and I see Jones was off his line. I thought, "That's in." It was one of those prophetic moments. I can't describe the feeling.'

It is an exceptional strike. And there are still 30 minutes to go. Will both teams try and shut up shop?

'None of it, they're going for the win,' says co-commentator, Andy Hinchcliffe.

It's frantic. It's end-to-end. Both teams have a couple of half chances, but neither can score. Not Orient. Not Rotherham. It goes to extra time. It goes to penalties.

Orient fans still struggle to talk about what happened next. Taking penalties towards the goal in front of their own fans, the Os are 3-2 up after the same number of penalties taken. On the brink of the Championship, they throw it away again. Missed attempts from defender Mathieu Baudry and substitute Chris Dagnall hand Rotherham the victory.

'Pure delirium at one end. Devastation and desolation at the other,' says Daniel Mann.

'Therapy kicks in from that point,' says Barry Hearn.

It would take a decade for the club to recover. Things would get far worse before they got better.

Fine lines

The 25,000 Orient fans walked away from Wembley that day, all devastated. All feeling slightly different about the future.

Paul Levy is a lifelong supporter. He presents the *Orient Outlook* podcast. He wasn't just devastated. He was angry.

'We're done,' he thought. 'It was just outright annoyance and frustration that we'd not done the job, considering we'd been in the top two for 75 or 80 per cent of the season. We just didn't manage the game well enough.'

Dave Victor, BBC Radio London's Orient correspondent, was slightly more positive, 'I felt relieved that we were there. I didn't take the run for granted. And I didn't know what was going to happen next. I thought that the Os would probably have another good season.'

Keren Harrison is the Leyton Orient Supporters' Club membership secretary and former supporter liaison officer for the club.

She said, 'I was completely gutted. I think I cried all that weekend. I felt like I was grieving for two weeks. I remember going back into work and somebody asked me who had died.'

Matt Simpson is a blogger, author, podcaster, and another lifelong fan. For Matt, Orient missed their chance. This was their time.

'It's the most gutted I've ever been as an Orient fan. That was our shot. It really felt like the stars were aligned for us. And in the penalty shoot-out ... I still thought we were going to do it. It just felt like it was our year.'

Manager Russell Slade was heartbroken.

'Fine lines, isn't it? We could have quite easily gone up, whether either winning it in 90, winning in extra time, or winning it on penalties. We were in it. And it was heartbreaking. Heartbreaking not to take this club up to the Championship.'

Alex Revell, who scored both Rotherham goals, reflected on his equaliser from 35 yards.

'It's what dreams are made of,' he said. 'The feeling when that hit the back of the net is one of pure jubilation.'

Fine lines, isn't it?

CHAPTER 1

Tears for years

Matt Porter was also at Wembley in 2014. He hasn't spoken about it since. 'I remember at the end, I went in the toilet and I just cried,' he tells me.

We're sitting in the academy office at Leyton Orient in autumn 2023. A midweek game, under the lights. It's the only room free. Club staff are buzzing around before the kick-off later that evening. A couple of squad players walk through as one of the investors sips a coffee before his next meeting.

Desks are messy, people are busy. Matt is the only person with nothing to do tonight. Even if he did have something to do, he's the sort of person who would make time to chat. Chief executive under Barry Hearn in 2014 (the youngest CEO in English football when he was appointed in 2006 at 26 years old), he's once again a key member of the Leyton Orient board. He first got a season ticket in 1995/96, under Hearn's famous £10 for under-16 season tickets. He loves this club.

We dive straight in. Wembley, 2014.

'You know, I still don't talk about it now. Just heartbreaking, just heartbreaking. If there was ever something that the club deserved to have, it was that. You know? And we just threw it away.'

At this point, Matt is holding back the tears, his voice choking as he revisits that day at Wembley.

'It's just horrific. I didn't watch Rotherham come up the stairs. I couldn't do it.'

The tears come now. And even though every Orient fan was hit hard by the result, for Matt the defeat was even more poignant. He'd been talking to Hearn, his boss and mentor. He knew what was coming next.

'I knew it was over. I knew it was done. You just felt like everything was being ripped away. We knew that was our last game regardless of what happened. Obviously, I didn't know how things were going to go.'

All he knew was that his boss had made a decision.

Barry Hearn was selling Leyton Orient.

2

'An absolute nutcase'

Barry Hearn on Francesco Becchetti, December 2023

'This guy is not here to mess about'
Thursday, 10 July 2014, press room, Brisbane Road
It had already been announced, but this made it official.

'Today, I suppose, is the end of an era and the birth of a new era.'

Nearly seven weeks after Wembley, Barry Hearn is speaking to the assembled media in the briefing room at Leyton Orient. It's a warm July day and the press room is packed. Alongside Hearn sits a man nobody recognises. Hearn is in a trademark pinstripe suit, blue tie. He's always well presented, white hair trimmed in a 'good enough for the school photo' sort of way – the consummate businessman. The other man, Francesco Becchetti, wears a black suit jacket with open collar. He has greying hair and a goatee beard. He says nothing as Hearn sets the scene. As ever, Hearn holds the room.

'Today we're here to announce and to confirm [that] the acquisition of Matchroom Sport's 90 per cent shareholding in Leyton Orient Football Club has been acquired by Mr Becchetti and his family interests.'

And so the new era begins.

As ever, Hearn is honest with his feelings for a club he saved almost two decades previously.

'It's been 20 years of my life. Twenty years that I have had aggravation, disappointment, excitement, controversy and a whole load of fun… I've enjoyed every second with this club … I think now, as a fan, I'm more excited than I've been for 20 years.'

No supporter can truly doubt Hearn's love for Orient. He's always been a pragmatic owner, a businessman first and foremost, but Orient has been his folly. A passion that goes against all his natural business instincts. In the 19 years he has owned the club he has made a small profit twice, broken even twice and lost money for 15 years. As he reiterates to the waiting press, 'I've always been consistent in saying the moment I find someone, in my view, that can take this club further than I can, I'm out.'

This isn't a rash decision.

'After six, seven, eight, different approaches from various companies over the past ten years, none of which have ticked my boxes, I suddenly find a man that ticks all my boxes. And I'm very, very happy to hand over the custodianship of this great club to Francesco.'

There is a moment in Hearn's speech where he stumbles over how to describe the new owner, touching his arm and smiling, as Becchetti pats his hand in return, 'I listen to this … er, friend on my right and I look into his eyes and I see a little bit of Barry Hearn, 20 years ago. He has excitement, he has vision, he has enthusiasm. But most of all, as all Italians have, he has a wealth of passion. This guy is not here to mess about.'

It's not an awkward moment, but it's one that you notice. Hearn understands this club. He knows how important good ownership is. He wants us to know he knows.

'I want to leave you with this thought. This football club is 132 years old. It's been an integral part of the East End of London for its entire existence. We are all just custodians of taking this club to the next level ... I'm totally and completely supportive of Francesco and his team. I'm looking forward to an amazingly successful and certainly a very different Leyton Orient football club.'

What was to come was certainly very different.

Are you close to Mayfair?

Hearn describes first being introduced to several people purporting to represent a 'mad Italian' in early 2014, maybe late 2013. When he eventually met him in person, Becchetti, who was 'extremely excitable', arrived with his mum.

'The only thing he kept saying was what I wanted to hear,' says Hearn. '"I'm going to put so much money into this club. We're going to be successful."'

After the wannabes with no money, this was a legitimate option for Hearn. 'The idea with Leyton Orient was not ever to stay there forever, but to leave a legacy,' he says. Having bought and developed the ground, making sure the club were able to rent it on a long lease ('I wouldn't be sitting here talking to you now if I'd have let Becchetti have the ground'), Hearn had taken the club as far as he was prepared to take it.

The deal was done long before the 2014 play-off final had even kicked off. The negotiations with Becchetti were almost as entertaining as the football.

'They were hilarious,' says Hearn. 'At one stage he went into a complete tantrum with my lawyers. His language was appalling. He's screaming. His eyes were rolling. And I said to Francesco, "You have to stop this now, because two things are going to happen. One is you're going to have a heart attack. Look at the state you're in. And secondly, if you talk to my people like that again, I'm going to knock you spark out." He stormed out the building, and I thought, "We'll never see him again." The following day, he turned up as if nothing had happened.'

Hearn remembers Becchetti initially being interested in Leyton Orient because he thought it was close to Mayfair, on the other side of London. 'He said, "Are you close to Mayfair?" I went, "Yeah, quite close on the underground." He went, "Oh, that's good." He was convinced that Orient was within walking distance from Mayfair!' In every sense, Leyton couldn't be further away.

Hearn admits that the longer the process went on, the more doubts he had about the potential new owner.

'I disliked him more and more during the conversations. And my right-hand man, Steve Dawson, used to just hold my leg down and whisper, "This is your exit." So, we shook hands on the deal.'

Becchetti agreed to buy Leyton Orient for £4m, promising to invest millions into the club. Barry Hearn, being Barry Hearn, couldn't resist one last gamble.

'I said to him, "You know, I think the deal's not great. I think I need some more money off you ... You're a billionaire, aren't you? Let's toss a coin for a half a million pound. If the good Lord decides I'm right and it's worth four and a half, not four, I'll win. And if the good Lord decides I'm greedy, I'll lose."

Becchetti declined – 'he absolutely shit himself!' – and the deal was done. 'I believe every single fan was happy that happened,' says Hearn. 'On that day, Becchetti got a hero's welcome. Every football fan's dream is to have a sugar daddy that's going to pile in the money.'

But who was Francesco Becchetti? And where did the money come from?

Links to waste management

It's been a decade, and we still don't know the real Francesco Becchetti. Many Orient fans still won't speak his name. He's the Voldemort of football. He who must not be named.

CHAPTER 2

In 2014, Becchetti was simply 'an Italian businessman' with links to 'waste management'. We know he had no previous experience running a football club and it's been widely reported since that he was on the run from Albania due to accusations of money laundering. Matt Simpson and James Masters, in their illuminating podcast *The Circus Upstairs*, which documents Becchetti's time at Orient, recall rumours that he owned a netball team. And that's about it.

Becchetti didn't give anyone many clues to his background at the press conference with Hearn. Talking through an interpreter, his first words immediately contradict his predecessor.

'I would like to correct Barry, because an era is not finishing, and a new era is not beginning. We are continuing with ever more strength in the history of Leyton Orient.'

After an odd turn of phrase and interpretation through the translator ('I have found everything clean from the point of view of management') he acknowledges the importance of continuity with manager Russell Slade.

'We renew and reiterate the confirmation of how much we appreciate Russell's contribution, and we have worked almost all night with new transfers, and in the next few hours we will have a few announcements to make.'

Watching the press conference now, it's hard not to interpret Hearn's movements and slight winces as someone slightly uncomfortable with the man sitting next to him.

'I knew there was something wrong with Becchetti the very first day I met him,' says Hearn. 'I didn't understand his background. I didn't understand his business. I didn't understand why his mum was sat in the corner. As the period of negotiations went on, I liked him less and less. The press conference was embarrassing. I realised what the club meant to me. And clearly, he was like a fish out of water. Money doesn't necessarily give you brains.'

Matt Porter watched on. Like everyone else, he was in the dark about his new boss.

'I didn't know a lot about him. I was the chief exec. I was in charge of the operations of the football club. Those negotiations were way over my head in terms of my ability as a business person back then. I'd never sold a business over millions of pounds. So, I'm not passing the buck or absolving myself of responsibility. But I'm also being honest about my involvement, which was very limited.'

Behind the scenes, meanwhile, Porter was already scrabbling around, trying to keep the wheels turning. He had stepped down from his role as chief executive, his role immediately reduced by Becchetti as part of the new owner's grand plan.

'He had a handshake with me and Barry that I would stay for a year to help with the transition. But it was clearly apparent that I was of no use to him other than the fact I was a signatory of official club documents.'

Did Becchetti know he was out of his depth?

'He didn't really think about it,' says Porter. 'He thought he was buying a football team, not a football club. And there is a major, major fundamental difference. He just thought, I'm just going to throw some money at it, sign some players. We're going to win every game. The rest of it just runs itself.'

Sounds easy, right?

There literally is only one Orient

Let's pause and take a walk down Leyton High Street.

Unless you support Orient or you've lived in Waltham Forest, most people don't really know much about Leyton. It's traditionally the non-trendy part of east London. You'll know that Shoreditch is stags, hens and office parties; Dalston is grubby and achingly cool; Broadway Market and Victoria Park 'village' are leafy fashion parades. If you can afford to

CHAPTER 2

stay in town, Walthamstow is where you go when you want to buy a place and have a baby. All fun places to be, but none of them are Leyton. None of them have London's second-oldest football club right in the heart of the community, hidden away behind rows of terraced houses.

Walking out of the tube, you see the legacy of the 2012 Olympics to the west; West Ham's London Stadium. So, you turn right, crossing the A12, the trunk road that connects old Cockney London with Essex and walk down the High Street. On matchday, there are blokes doing their matchday walk. Heads down, feet moving frantically, skipping around traffic. They've got somewhere to be. There's no merchandise being sold, no half-and-half scarves. This is a working high street that gets you to a football match.

Normal people still live in Leyton. People who support the club and people who have never even thought about attending a match. Students and young professionals have started moving in as well. It's on the Central line. It's cheaper than the fashion parades. It's got a restaurant called Five Lads. And a KFC imitation called GFC (Great Fried Chicken).

As you shuffle down the High Street, you might stop in at Kapture, the cocktail and wine bar that also serves beer, unless of course it's been taken over by a particularly rowdy away support. In which case you'll skip on, maybe stopping for a pre-match meal in Figo's Italian, although you'll probably need to book nowadays. Some people will head to the Lion and Key, or the Leyton Star, but if you can get there early enough, you could find yourself in the Coach and Horses, a pub with Orient programs from glory days past wallpapered to the toilet walls.

You can see the stadium, the back of the old East Stand (and it is *old*, originally installed in 1955) down the terraced street, running along Brisbane Road. You'll look in at Coronation Gardens, a green space behind the ground where the statue of Laurie Cunningham stands. An Orient and West Bromwich Albion legend, he was the first British player to play for Real Madrid, and the first black player to represent England at any level when he played in an under-21 international. People pose for photos next to him.

Leyton Orient are proud of their history. As any supporter will tell you there are plenty of Towns, Cities and Uniteds, but there's only one Orient. Named after the Orient Steamship & Navigation Company's *SS Orient* (after a suggestion from a player and Orient Steamship employee in the late 19th century), the club has been around since 1881. In that time, Orient have been in the top division of English football just once (1962/63, relegated after one season), have reached one FA Cup semi-final (fans of a certain age will tell you all about Peter Kitchen – you can watch his heroics on YouTube) and after a steady period in the second tier through the 1960s and 70s have bounced around the third and fourth levels ever since.

2014 was supposed to be the dawning of a golden age.

* * *

I was first taken to Orient by my mate in the mid-90s. Like Matt Porter I got a ridiculously cheap season ticket as an under-16. I'd grown up a Cockney red, a Manchester United fan like my dad and granddad, basking in the glory of the class of '92 from afar. Orient were always 'the team I go and watch'. Like many people in London and the surrounding towns, they were my second team. Over time, that changed. Going to matches week in, week out, you can't not start to care. Soon your second team becomes your first team, and you wonder why you ever had an affinity with a global mega brand 200 miles away that you only go and see a few times a year (to be fair, my dad took me to loads of United away games in London in the 90s because you could still get tickets, but that soon changed).

CHAPTER 2

Like myself, Mark Hannah grew up supporting a different team. I first met Mark away at Bristol Rovers in 2021. I say meet, I saw this Scottish lad in his 20s tumble down the terraces and crack his head open while celebrating a goal in a 3-1 Orient victory. When he woke up in a Bristol hospital, it was to a barrage of messages and concern from the Orient family.

Growing up in Leith, Edinburgh, five minutes from Hibernian's Easter Road, Mark was a Rangers fan by virtue of his dad's allegiance. He never really felt like Rangers were his team, and he couldn't support Hibs or Hearts due to his inherited affection for Rangers. For most of his life, he was looking for a sense of football community. A club he could call his own. In 2019 he gained a scholarship to the London Academy of Music and Dramatic Art. At the age of 24, he moved down south. He could have chosen any London club. He chose Leyton Orient.

'Coming from the environment that I'm from, I've grown up in places like the Hibernian Supporters' Club ... social clubs in Edinburgh. I thought, I need something like that, because I have to keep in touch, keep the reality of that world I know so well.'

On his first trip to Orient, he walked the wrong way out of the tube, turned around, walked into the away fans' pub, walked out again, eventually found his way to the ground and was shocked that there were flats everywhere (uniquely, the corners of Brisbane Road are filled in with private flats that overlook the pitch). Eventually he found the supporters' club. He never looked back.

'I got myself a bottle of Becks and just kind of stood sheepishly.'

It didn't take long for him to find himself in conversation with a supporters' club regular, a man with an Orient tattoo on his leg.

In a country full of Towns, Roads and Uniteds, there is only one Orient.

'I was feeling quite brave. I just candidly approached him and said, "That's amazing. Can I take a photograph of your leg?" And he was like, "Yeah, yeah. Absolutely." And we got chatting and he was like, "Oh, you're not from around here." I said, "No, no, no. This is my first Leyton Orient game." And he was like, "Oh, what? You need to meet *everyone*." And so then gradually, over those coming weeks, I got to know everyone at that club.'

Orient fans always talk about how friendly the club is, how welcoming. Mark lived and breathed that hospitality.

'I'm a living example of that. I'm not from the area. But when you're Orient – that's it. I was very conscious going in – "Right, I'm an outsider. And this might be quite difficult." But it totally wasn't. I needn't have worried. It was incredible.'

The Orient community welcomes everyone.

No wonder Becchetti wanted to buy it.

3

Summer, 2014.

Largely the same squad walk into the training ground at Chigwell for pre-season training at the start of the 2014/15 season. The only major departure is Moses Odubajo, who leaves for Brentford for a reported £1m fee. Russell Slade is backed by the fans and his players to go again.

Shopping at Harrods, staying at the Dorchester

'The mood was excited,' admits captain Nathan Clarke, speaking a few years later. 'There was a good buzz going back.'

The team had every reason to believe. After all, this was the same group of lads who had come so close just a few months earlier. This would be Orient's year.

Some Championship-level experience made its way through the door to boost the team's chances. Signings like Jobi McAnuff, Darius Henderson and Jay Simpson looked to be another step forward. As Russell Slade said, with Francesco Becchetti's waste-management money sloshing around, 'I can now be shopping at Harrods rather than Primark.'

What Slade didn't necessarily need was a new sporting director. Mauro Milanese, former Premier League defender and a man who spent much of the 1990s playing in Italy's

Serie A, was parachuted in by Becchetti. His remit: to run the football side of the club. A remit that, up until that moment, Slade had been running.

'From a distance, it looked to make sense,' says BBC London Sport's Dave Victor. 'But you wouldn't give it to somebody who isn't actually a sporting director. He [Milanese] was just an Italian international. He wasn't a sporting director. He was an ex-player. I don't think he thought like a manager or a coach or a sporting director. His interest was himself.'

As Victor states, a director of football or sporting director is nothing unusual. At all levels of football, many clubs have the role in place – a partnership between manager and director is something that modern managers expect. It wasn't necessarily a strange move for Becchetti to make.

What was strange were the rumours that Milanese's London residence was the Dorchester Hotel. And rather than travelling with the squad on the team coach, or driving himself, he was taken to a pre-season friendly at Northampton in a private car. The car then waited until after the match and took him back down the A1 to the Dorchester. Not the life of a director of football for a tier-three club. At best, it was a naive use of club money.

Silly money was being splashed, or attempting to be splashed, in other areas too. Stories floated around about the owner putting pressure on Slade to bring in players on wages that wouldn't be out of place in the Premier League. At one point, former Newcastle United striker Leon Best was approached. He was on £39,000 per week.

'The recruitment was so haphazard,' says Matt Porter. 'At the time, our top-paid player was earning £2,200 a week. And then they went and signed three players who earned more than £8,000 a week. A load more who were earning £4,000 a week. They didn't give any of the players who got to the play-off final new contracts. So straight away, that harmony, that team spirit, that collective response, that collective spirit ... it was all undermined.'

Porter is quick to point out that this disharmony wasn't the fault of the new signings, but the owner had made his mark.

Becchetti took things further by attempting to change the team's win bonus scheme, a sacred document that each member of the squad signs up to. Porter recalls the incident happening on the Thursday immediately before the new season started.

'He walked into the training ground and gave the team a sheet of paper and said, "Sign this." And they're like, "Well, we can't. We've got to talk to the PFA. We've got to talk to each other." So, they're starting to get a little bit suspicious. Scared, maybe.'

The senior members of the squad trusted Porter, though. They asked him to speak to Becchetti. To see if he could sort it out.

'I saw him the next day, and I had a piece of paper in my hand. He was sat at the boardroom table. I just put it on the table in front of him. I said, "Sign that." He just looked up at me, all startled. And I said, "That's what you've just done to the players, and you're surprised they won't sign it." And he just fobbed me off. He wasn't interested. It didn't have any impact. He wasn't there to listen to me.'

Becchetti wasn't there to listen to anyone. Not Porter, not the players.

And certainly not the fans.

Leyton Calling

Becchetti's first season didn't start well. After six matches, Orient sat in 18th position, towards the bottom of League One. Worryingly, there were also rumours floating around of unrest behind the scenes. Nobody knew what was going on. It was a strange time to be an Orient fan.

'I feel like I'm in therapy,' says Paul Levy when I bring up those early days under Becchetti.

When Paul and his mate Steve Nussbaum (another pair from the £10 season ticket generation of the 90s) launched *The Orient Outlook Podcast* in February 2014, the club were second in League One. Promotion beckoned. Anything was possible. But after the poor start the following season, and the talk of disgruntlement at the club, everything changed. Paul and Steve suddenly found themselves broadcasting from the front line. Figureheads in an underground revolution, fighting against the waves of misinformation that were drip fed from the club's official channels.

They were part of the Orient resistance, secretly broadcasting the truth.

'That's a mad analogy, but yeah, absolutely,' says Paul. 'Like living in a country where it's state-run media. The club put out what they were allowed to put out. The information coming out of the club in the early days was piecemeal. And this is no reflection on the media team at the time, but it was just poorly put out because of what the owners wanted. How they wanted it drip-fed out to the fanbase. Keep them in the dark as much as you can. Don't tell them anything.'

Paul is keen to keep his sources secret, but his contacts in the club were doing their best to keep the fans informed of the truth.

'We had *people*, thankfully. People on the inside who felt the fans ought to know what was going on, how it was going on, and the fact that they were still doing their best in terrible circumstances. And we're very, very, very grateful to them. They helped keep the fanbase, I say sane … sane in terms of the truth of what was going on. But not really *that* sane, because what was going on was pretty crazy.'

CHAPTER 3

In his early 40s, a lifelong Orient fan, he's proud of his role in keeping the fanbase as informed as he could. He was a man who just wanted to start a podcast with his mate, to chat about his football club and hopefully see them get promoted. He didn't sign up for this.

Listening to those early podcasts (they've now released well over 300), broadcasting as the new owners made their mark, Paul and Steve are surprisingly calm given the unexpected circumstances, guiding a worried fanbase through a time of real anxiety and confusion. They're not reflecting on a week's football. They're broadcasting about a crisis.

Take an episode from September 2014. It starts, 'Another chaotic week in the life of a Leyton Orient fan … every week we think we'll have trouble filling half an hour. But every week we struggle to stay within the half-hour, because so much is happening … Crazy week.'

'It was such a responsibility,' says Paul. 'To be putting information out there where you're criticising players, because they haven't done very well, or they've not done their best. But not necessarily always understanding what was going on behind the scenes.'

But did anyone really know what was going on? On 13 September, after a league defeat at home to Colchester, a clue to the unrest leaked to the world, via *Orient Outlook*.

It came straight out of the manager's mouth.

Curtains
Saturday, 13 September 2014, Brisbane Road
League One, Leyton Orient 0 Colchester United 2

They call it the A12 derby, but it's just another Saturday 3pm kick-off. There's slightly raised stakes, but it's not Spurs-Arsenal. However, it was the start of two games and two incidents that have become Orient folklore.

Paul Levy and Steve Nussbaum were lucky enough to be pitchside following the home defeat to Colchester, part of the media representatives recording the post-match interview with manager Russell Slade and BBC Radio London correspondent Dave Victor.

'My eyes were almost popping out of my head,' said Paul, at the time. 'I wasn't sure if I was hearing him right. It was one of them shock moments.'

What they discovered they put straight out on their social channels:

'The president's been honest enough, via Mauro Milanese, to tell us we've got one game to sort it out,' says Slade, in the interview. 'The situation is we need to get a win on Tuesday [away at Notts County], or it will be curtains.'

As Slade made his way back down the tunnel, the assembled media didn't know what to do. Directors of football don't enter the changing room and give the manager ultimatums straight after a match. Football managers don't come out and repeat exactly what was said to them to the media. It's unprecedented.

'Me and Paul were standing there looking a bit gormless,' says Steve, talking through the incident on his podcast. 'We were bemused.'

The situation was unbelievable. Slade had to win at Meadow Lane or he would lose his job. As Paul and Steve tweeted, then followed up with the full interview in their podcast, fans like Matt Simpson of *The Circus Upstairs* could finally see what was happening. Things were falling apart rapidly.

'We'd drawn a couple that we should have probably won, and it was sort of fine,' says Matt. 'There was absolutely no justification for issuing an ultimatum to Slade. It just made me realise that we're in for a very different type of ownership. I really valued the fact that Barry Hearn had been very loyal to managers. These were the first sort of alarm bells.'

CHAPTER 3

A few days later, Orient travelled to Notts County for the make-or-break game for Slade's management. Slade's team didn't beat the Magpies. But nor did they lose. The resulting 1-1 draw left nobody sure what that meant for the manager.

Dave Victor stayed around after the match to try to find out what was happening. By the time Slade emerged from the bowels of Meadow Lane, after a prolonged meeting with Francesco Becchetti, the ground was empty. All the lights had been turned off.

'It was probably half 11, quarter to 12 before he came out and I did an interview. And I knew something had happened,' said Dave.

Speaking to *The Circus Upstairs*, Dave describes the scene. 'What happened at Meadow Lane that night was very, very peculiar ... Russell came out and explained that they'd had a meeting and that they'd cleared the air, and that he thought he was still the manager of Leyton Orient.'

Dave took his news to social media. Like Paul and Steve on the *Orient Outlook* socials a few days before, the announcement raced through the fanbase.

'Twitter was in its early days,' he tells me. 'I got 43,000 likes or something. It was ridiculous. I was the only person that broke the news that Russell had had the meeting with the chairman and was staying in the job.'

Was Slade angry at the time?

'No. I think he *thought* he'd had a proper meeting, but I don't think anybody had a proper meeting with him [Becchetti] because he was just such a strange man.'

Things got even stranger a few days later. In the programme notes before the home League Cup tie against Sheffield United the following Tuesday, Becchetti addressed the Orient fans with his account of recent events. 'At the end of the [Colchester] game I sent Mauro Milanese into the locker room to express the disappointment with the leadership on the defeat. The message was, "If with the next match there was no redemption we would be forced to remove Russell Slade from his position and our responsibility will be with the team itself."

'Just after Mauro Milanese left the changing room, I saw that Russell Slade repeated to the press what was said in the changing room. I have to say it left me very puzzled, because as I have always believed that anything said in the changing room is covered by secrecy. Enshrined in an iron pact of invincibility between players, the coach and the club.

'In families, husbands and wives quarrel often, and sometimes they say they will leave and usually they remain together. Or parents threaten to spank their children, but usually do not carry out the threat.

'In that moment I felt I have to give a wake-up jolt. But for me, it's wrong to dismiss a coach during the season, and even then, I would only do it in extreme cases. In fact, the team did not win the game on Tuesday, but I did not relieve Russell of his post. Regardless of the pressure from the press and you.'

The Sheffield United match ended in a 1-0 defeat, but it probably didn't make a difference. A few days later, Slade resigned, citing 'a breakdown in the relationship with the new owners'.

He wouldn't be the last ex-manager to cite a breakdown with Becchetti and his team.

'They're a good group, Dave'

Dave Victor meets me in the supporters' club. It's almost nine years to the day after Notts County in 2014 and the club hasn't changed much. It's exactly as you'd expect; friendly, carpeted, full of Orient fans of a certain age. The club are very proud of their real ales and welcoming environment. I settle in with a pint and chat to a couple of faces I know, but

CHAPTER 3

it's too loud to do an interview, everyone dissecting the match we've just seen. Dave knows this will be the case. Thankfully, he's sorted a space up in the gallery overlooking the pitch for our interview.

After a brief dalliance with West Ham ('I was born in '57. So the first game my dad took me to was Upton Park. It was just after West Ham won the World Cup') he came to Brisbane Road. It was 1971, racism on the terraces was rife. But Orient felt different. He didn't look back.

'The team looked different because there were black players. You know, in the 70s, it was horrible. But the atmosphere felt different [at Brisbane Road]. It wasn't without its racism, but it was so different to everywhere else in London at the time. This just felt like a home.'

For Dave, the problems of Becchetti's first season had started well before September, the Colchester ultimatum and Notts County away. In tune with the way Russell Slade built a team, Dave immediately recognised that something wasn't quite right when the club signed former Premier League striker Darius Henderson.

'Some of the signings in the summer I thought were OK. The one I worried about, and the one I thought, "Well, that's not a Russell signing," was Henderson. You know, Russell would say to us, "They're a good group, Dave. They're a good group. They're good characters." I thought, "I'm not sure this lot coming in now are." I'm not sure they were Russell's lads. I know he would have signed other players.'

Alongside the signing of Henderson, two pre-season matches raised red flags for Dave.

'I can remember we played at Dartmouth, a pre-season friendly. It was an unusual game because it was stopped because of a thunderstorm. It finished early. So I'm interviewing Russell and he's saying, "Well, I could get used to working with a sporting director. [But] it doesn't sit easy."

All this sort of stuff. And it had been a really odd summer. They hadn't done any pre-season preparations. The games we played were really odd, and they didn't go abroad. It was all obviously done at the last minute. And they booked a hotel in the north-east. So, our second and probably our most significant pre-season friendly was at Gateshead.'

There's nothing unusual in a League One club playing a friendly against a non-league team like Gateshead during pre-season. But normally a club like Leyton Orient would play against a local non-league team. Bishop's Stortford, Billericay, Potters Bar. They wouldn't travel almost 300 miles to the north-east to take on Gateshead on a Tuesday night. It was, to say the least, a strange decision.

'When I got there, you could cut the atmosphere with a knife,' says Dave. 'The players were so miserable. And obviously, the hotel wasn't great. This was their pre-season. And it couldn't have been worse.'

Events after the match soon cemented Dave's suspicions that Slade was being undermined by the new regime. Sitting in a cafe ('It's really uncomfortable, not very nice') with the squad, the Orient press officer asked Dave if he could give striker David Mooney a lift home. Mooney's wife was heavily pregnant, and he wanted to get back as soon as possible to be with her. It's the sort of task Dave would often undertake to support the team.

'Normally Russell would come over and say, "Thank you very much," and you'd just jump in the car and go. But we're sitting there and there was this tall, dark figure dressed very strangely in the background. I'm waiting for a decision. I'm still sitting there and it's uncomfortable. They were obviously waiting for the sporting director to give the nod. In the end, we were allowed to go. But it clearly wasn't Russell's decision. And that really struck me as odd.'

It was a season of odd incidents.

CHAPTER 3

He's got no hair, but we don't care

I manage to catch Russell Slade at a book signing. We're in the club shop before a home match in November and for the first time this season, it's properly cold outside. Slade has joined a line-up of Orient legends on a long table at the back of the shop, signing copies of the recently released *Leyton Orient – Official History Book, 1881–2023*.

The shop is busy, a steady stream of local fans and curious Americans making Thanksgiving purchases. A boy of about six or seven walks around with his new home shirt, trying to persuade his amused grandparents that his 'baby sister' would love a mini football. He's pushing his luck – he's already been bought a stuffed Wyvern toy (Theo and Cleo are the Orient club mascots, both two-legged winged dragons). Still, he gets his little football.

Among the replica shirts and scarfs, the range of 'Leyton Orient Pointing Gnomes' gets a surprising amount of attention. 'You can't go wrong with an Orient gnome, I suppose,' says one fan.

As the queue for signatures dies down slightly, Russell and I grab a couple of minutes at the back of the shop. He's softly spoken, warm, engaging. I ask how Becchetti and Milanese's behaviour affected him and his team. How was he feeling at the time?

'Listen, you're a football manager. You're there to do your job. You try to ignore all of that. And the changing rooms are a very important place. And it's important that that group stayed together. That group did stay together.'

He's a much-respected manager and it's almost impossible to mention Slade to a group of Orient supporters without one of them replying with the affectionate chant, 'He's got no hair, but we don't care.' The players enjoyed working with him, the staff admired him, and the fans loved him. And that night at Notts County, almost a decade before our chat, the fans had turned up in numbers. At the end of the match, Slade applauded them for it. Becchetti objected.

'It was one of the most emotional games for me,' says Slade. 'So many fans turned up. And when I saw him [Becchetti] afterwards, he asked me why I went over to the fans. I said, "Because they spend an awful lot of money. I've got a great relationship with them. I want to applaud them and thank them for coming all this way."

'"No, don't do that. [Becchetti said] Don't do that. I don't want you to do that again." I said, "But I will." And then he went on about the game. I asked him what he wanted to do. "You want to get rid of me? I'm ready to go if that's what you want." The conversations were, in the end, very, very straightforward and blunt. I'd lost any little respect I'd had for him, really.'

I leave Slade to it. The official club photographer is trying to organise a photo. And everyone wants a piece of him. When long-serving kit manager Ada Martin pops in to say hi, he's greeted with an affectionate hug and a 'heyyyyy how are you?!' from Slade. Everyone is happy to see their former boss.

The way he was treated by the Becchetti regime is still impossible for everyone to understand.

'My dog could have negotiated a better deal!'

It will get madder. But it's worth taking a moment to remember what was going on in 2014. As Dave Victor explains, 'Context is important.'

Two years earlier the London Olympics had taken place on Orient's doorstep – the Olympic Stadium in plain sight from Leyton High Street. According to Barry Hearn, the original post-Olympics plan was to turn the Olympic Stadium into a 20,000-capacity ground, perfect for Leyton Orient to move into. It was something that both the mayor

CHAPTER 3

of London, Ken Livingstone, and Olympics minister Tessa Jowell envisioned. It made sense for all parties. However, by the time the Olympics came around, and Boris Johnson was mayor of London, the stadium plans had changed. It was going to remain a 50-to-60,000-seat arena. West Ham were interested in moving in.

Hearn was keen for a groundshare between West Ham and Orient, but Karren Brady, the Hammers' chief executive, wanted the stadium exclusively for her club. What followed was a protracted legal battle, as Brady negotiated what Hearn describes as 'the deal of the century' – securing sole occupancy of the Olympic Stadium for a small annual rent with matches funded at great expense by the public.

As Hearn said in 2016, the year West Ham finally moved in, 'My dog could have negotiated a better deal for the taxpayer.'

Like many people associated with Leyton Orient, Dave Victor was very worried about West Ham's impending move. In 2014 it was more of a concern than Hearn selling the club to Becchetti. The fear was that the West Ham stadium would be such a draw for paying punters that it would crush little old Leyton Orient.

'The concern at the time wasn't anything other than West Ham,' says Dave. 'I thought the West Ham move was going to have such an impact on the club. And I thought the impact would be much greater than it was.'

Maybe Becchetti could help resist the threat of West Ham's move? After all, here was a man prepared to invest the money that Hearn never could. Maybe he could take Orient to the next level?

'Barry didn't have a Championship budget,' explains Dave. 'And there seemed to be an opportunity. There might not be a little old Orient in the future. There might be a bigger project here.'

By the time Becchetti was in control, the West Ham stadium deal had been long done. Orient's Olympic Stadium ambitions were not on the table. But Becchetti's takeover still made logical sense for many, including Dave.

'When the deal was done, I thought, "Well, you know, this looks good." I know Barry wasn't going to spend any of his own money if we'd gone into the Championship, it was going to be a struggle. But it wouldn't have been with somebody with big pockets, you know? And the bloke spent money, didn't he?'

Yes. The bloke spent money. Becchetti spent a lot of money. The problem was, Orient hadn't made it into the Championship.

They were heading in the other direction.

4

It is the last game of the 2014/15 season. Leyton Orient are on the brink of relegation back to League Two for the first time in almost a decade. It has been a disastrous year. Russell Slade's replacement, Kevin Nugent, was sacked within three months of his appointment. Former Italian international Fabio Liverani is put in charge until the end of the season. He oversees a troubled campaign, marked by rumours of interference in team selection from president Francesco Becchetti and sporting director Mauro Milanese. Orient have to win away against Swindon Town to stand any chance of avoiding relegation.

Catastrophic mismanagement
Sunday, 3 May 2015, County Ground, Swindon
Swindon Town 2 Leyton Orient 2

Almost a year after the heartbreak of Wembley, there was heartbreak again. Leyton Orient were relegated from League One. After being so close to the Championship, the second tier of English football, the club were back in the fourth tier. It was a shocking 12 months.

The performance at Swindon reflected the mood in the club. Losing a two-goal lead to a second-string Swindon team of ten men, Orient limped towards relegation with a

2-2 draw. As it turns out, other results went against them. Even if they'd won, they wouldn't have made it.

Dave Victor is scathing, 'I've seen some dire performances over the years, dire. But the worst beyond doubt was Swindon. Because Swindon were in the play-offs. They really didn't want to play. And they played terrible. And that [Orient] performance was beyond bad. It was kids playing in that Swindon team and we couldn't even beat them.'

There had been off-field distractions (more, *much* more, on this soon), but the team never recovered from the disruption of the start of the season. The disparity in wages between the new arrivals and the tight-knit group of players that had reached the play-off final, three different managers, a language barrier, a former Italian international in Fabio Liverani who spent most of his career playing in Italy's Serie A in charge of a third-tier English football club – all factors that contributed to an awful series of results.

For Dave, just getting a straight answer out of Liverani had proved problematic.

'It was impossible. I did these interviews, and the answer that he'd give would be really long, and then it would be translated, and it would be really short. And then I'd follow up the question and you could see on Fabio's face that he couldn't understand why I'd ask that question.'

Still, Dave feels that the appointment of Liverani could, maybe should, have worked out.

'I think something went wrong quite early doors with Fabio Liverani. And that's the bit that I think is interesting. Why didn't it work under him? Because he's clearly a good coach. I thought, "Well, actually, this makes sense." His CV, especially being the first black Italian international, you think, "Wow." [He was] a proper manager, a proper football man. And I have no idea if he was as difficult as he was because he wasn't allowed to pick the team or not.'

CHAPTER 4

Matt Porter had left the club back in September, invited out of the boardroom a year earlier than planned by the new chief executive, Alessandro Angelieri. For Porter, it was clear why things had gone so spectacularly wrong in Becchetti's first season.

'The mistake they made was not caring about the club. It was just about the team. Everything else has to work in order for the football team to work. If you don't get the structure of the club right and the personnel right, then you're not going to build a platform that players can succeed on. I put it in writing that I didn't agree with the documents I was signing. Things like some player contracts that were way too high, other documents where the club was wasting money or not doing the right thing. I'm not suggesting anything illegal, but just bad business.'

For the first time in 20 years, Porter stopped going to games. 'I just divorced myself from it completely. I didn't even look at who we were playing. Barely looked at the results.'

For regular fans like Matt Simpson, it was impossible to understand how such a collapse could have been allowed to happen. He was at the County Ground that day, as he'd been at Wembley 12 months earlier. His prediction that Orient had blown their golden chance in that play-off defeat was painfully accurate.

'I don't know why I even went [to Swindon]. I mean, it's almost the inverse of what I was feeling after the play-off final. I sort of knew that we were going to go down. I had seen no evidence over the last six months of football that we were going to do anything but go down. And you know, I was completely resigned to it. Imagine in any other walk of life mismanaging something that badly. It's insane. It's crazy. It's catastrophic mismanagement.'

Insane. Crazy. Catastrophic.

And it was nothing on what was to come.

You've heard of Agon TV, right?

It's time to talk about the nonsense. The off-field distractions. The madness. The insane, the crazy, the catastrophic.

In total, nine full-time managers served under Becchetti. All of them working while a world of incompetence bumbled on around them. It was a mess epitomised by what James Masters and Matt Simpson in their podcast, *The Circus Upstairs*, describe as the 'horror show' of the Leyton Orient reality TV series. A show simply titled *Leyton Orient*.

In late 2014 Becchetti launched his Albanian TV channel, Agon, on to Italian TV. His new reality show was to be a key fixture in the channel's schedule. The premise was simple. Twelve young Italian footballers competing for a professional contract with Leyton Orient, the players undertaking a series of challenges where each week one of the hopefuls is eliminated. Unfortunately, very little footage exists of the show. What does remain shows little more than an Albanian television studio with a surprisingly enthusiastic host, cut between shots of young Italian men freezing in tracksuit tops while sitting on the bench at Brisbane Road.

The disruption the filming caused was evident to everyone involved with the club, although maybe not the owners. *Welcome to Wrexham* it was not. The team were struggling.

Among the players filming a lip-sync video to 'The Best Day Of My Life' by rock(ish) band American Authors, the TV crew were filming their exploits on the training ground and around the stadium at Brisbane Road. They also regularly played practice matches on the pitch. As the show's director and producer, Alessandro Ugo, told *The Circus Upstairs* when explaining his role in proceedings, 'There was tension in the team. The team was not 100 per cent happy about a reality show being filmed.'

This was an understatement. Dave Victor saw the impact first hand.

CHAPTER 4

'I think it affected everybody. What was happening off the pitch felt for a while to be more important than what was happening on it. And I can remember the difficulties we had in the press box, there were so many cameras and so many crews, they just dominated everything. Football was almost a distraction at that point.'

For Dave, it was clear that Becchetti wasn't focused on what he should have been focusing on. 'His priority initially seemed to be the TV. People who were employed 24/7 at the club were told that the TV was the priority. You can't expect the focus to be on the starting 11 if everyone's been told, "The focus is this TV show." And it was dire. Absolute rubbish.'

In the end, there were two joint winners of the coveted Leyton Orient contract. But that was the last anyone heard of it. The lucky lads never became Orient players. Matt Simpson even wrote to chief executive Alessandro Angelieri on numerous occasions asking when the club were going to reveal the winners. After one or two replies saying that news was coming, Angelieri stopped replying.

'I was genuinely outraged by it,' Matt tells me. 'I just was really affronted by the fact that they'd spent, I assume, millions of pounds on this reality show where the whole point of it was the winner got a contract with Orient. And then they just never mentioned it again. And I was like, "I'm not letting that go. You have to explain why you're not going ahead with that."'

Like much that went on during the Becchetti regime, nothing was properly explained. And all of this took place in the first season of his ownership. It was just the start.

Honey and sliced meats

Harrods isn't necessarily a traditional venue for Leyton Orient players to do their weekly shop, but Andrea Dossena wasn't a traditional Leyton Orient player.

Once signed by Liverpool for a reported £7m, Dossena was also an Italian international and a man who scored against Manchester United at Old Trafford in the Premier League.

A few years later, in the November of Becchetti's first season, Dossena signed for Orient on a free transfer. He'd spent years playing for Napoli in Italy's Serie A. He'd played in the Europa League and the Champions League. It was much more of a surprise that he was playing in League One for Leyton Orient than shopping in Harrods.

Even more surprising were the reports in April 2015 that Dossena had been arrested for stealing some honey and sliced meats while shopping in Harrods with his family. It was just another bizarre turn in the mounting list of bizarre turns that were spinning around Becchetti's Orient.

Dossena's explanation, reported in *The Guardian*, is an equally bizarre read, 'I was in Harrods with my wife and my son for some shopping and I forgot to pay for a honey jar and some sliced meats we had previously ordered. While exiting the shop unaware of my oversight, I was stopped by security guards [who] then called the police as a standard routine procedure.

'As I wasn't carrying with me any identity documents at the time, I was asked to go to the nearest police station in order to be identified, after which I left and went back home. Hence, I have now instructed my lawyers to protect my image with all necessary legal actions against those who reported this inaccurate and tendentious news.'

The well-paid left-back was bailed and, ultimately, not prosecuted. But the reports *were* accurate. He *was* arrested on suspicion of stealing some honey and sliced meats. 'Oversight' or not, a Leyton Orient player was arrested in Harrods on suspicion of nicking a honey pot just a few months after Russell Slade's announcement that due to Becchetti's cash injection he could now shop for players 'at Harrods rather than Primark'.

As James Master says on *The Circus Upstairs*, it was a 'nice bit of symmetry' at least.

5

After Leyton Orient's relegation to League Two at the end of the 2014/15 season, Fabio Liverani is relieved of his duties. Becchetti appoints former Orient player Ian Hendon as manager. Hendon had previously served as a coach at West Ham under Sam Allardyce. For many associated with Orient, it is a sensible appointment.

In June, the Albanian government put out an arrest warrant for Becchetti and his mother. Accused of fraud-related offences and money laundering, they impound the Agon TV channel. Becchetti is later arrested in London. He is ordered to hand in his passport to the authorities.

In August, Leyton Orient win their first five league matches of the 2015/16 season.

They fail to win a single game in September.

'We did some mistakes'
Saturday, 5 September 2015, St James Park
Exeter City 4 Leyton Orient 0

All it took was one defeat for the nonsense to kick off again. But even before a 4-0 away defeat to Exeter at the start of September, things weren't ideal. A sensible managerial appointment in Ian Hendon alongside some sensible

CHAPTER 5

departures in the form of Andrea Dossena and fellow Italian Gianvito Plasmati, plus some sensible signings like future Wrexham striker Ollie Palmer from Mansfield, all indicated that the leadership team had learned some lessons from the previous season's profligacy. As Becchetti's chief executive Alessandro Angelieri said, 'We did some mistakes. We don't want to do the same mistakes.'

In reality, they had learned nothing. They did some more mistakes.

Jobi McAnuff was a gem of a player. Signed by Russell Slade in Becchetti's first summer, he had previously captained Reading to the Championship title, taking them into the Premier League. After his first season with Orient, and the club's relegation to League Two, he found himself playing with the youth team. It didn't make sense.

Speaking to *The Circus Upstairs*, Dave Victor recalls questioning Hendon on why McAnuff wasn't in the first-team squad.

'He said, "Dave, why do you keep asking me about Jobi?" I said, "Well, he's a big player, where is he? He said, "I can't tell you. I can't *tell* you I can't pick him. And don't ask me again." It was a real reflection on just how much control Ian had on the squad and what was happening.'

According to multiple reports from within the club, McAnuff had been singled out by Becchetti and his team as the scapegoat for the previous season's relegation. His punishment? To train with the youth team, unable to play first-team football, and unable to leave the club. McAnuff just had to get on with it.

McAnuff, now a respected television pundit, tells me what happened, 'I was told that I wasn't wanted at the football club any more, as soon as the season finished. Basically, it was "my fault" and some of the other players' fault that we got relegated. We "weren't team players". We "weren't contributing." I had a real issue with that. And I'm very clear to the chairman about this, which didn't go down very well in a meeting.'

McAnuff describes relegation the previous season as 'one of the lowest points of my career'. He had joined Orient to get them promoted. He certainly hadn't planned to be part of a squad that was relegated into League Two.

'Everybody at that football club didn't do enough that year,' he tells me. 'Were there excuses or reasons why? Maybe. But players let it affect them too much. Performance levels were nowhere near good enough. And we just had no togetherness, no real spirit. And that is unacceptable. And I mean that across the board. That's not one or two players in particular. It was just a bad place to be. So obviously, relegation occurred. I was absolutely gutted. But I did feel responsible. I wasn't anywhere near my best in that year for the club. And I wanted to stay and try and make things better.'

At his best or not, Becchetti questioning his commitment was something McAnuff could not accept.

'Any fan who said "I wasn't at my best" – I absolutely have to take that on the chin, because I wasn't. It happens at times, for whatever reason. But in terms of questioning my character and my attitude and what I was doing around the group, that's something I would never, ever accept from anyone. So, I made a point of saying to him [Becchetti] that I didn't accept it. I said to him, "Listen, you go and speak to every single player in that dressing room, and you ask them if I've been a good pro, if I've tried to drive the group, regardless of how well I'm playing on a Saturday or Tuesday. Not one of them can tell me that I wasn't a good team-mate, not one."

His pleas made no difference. To make things worse, Becchetti refused to communicate his decision. Understandably, McAnuff was deeply troubled.

CHAPTER 5

'All of a sudden, I'm now in a position where I'm not playing. Maybe it looks to people as if I've said, "Well, that's it. I don't want to play for Leyton Orient," which was nonsense.'

With a young family, uprooting and finding a new club was the last thing McAnuff wanted to do. However, funding the necessary insurance and travel himself, he went on trial to Bolton and Blackburn. Nothing came of it, and McAnuff found himself stuck in a contract at Leyton Orient, unable to play. A professional footballer, in a professional prison, through no fault of his own.

'In the end, I sort of came back, got my head down,' he says. 'Ian Hendon was fantastic. He was trying to mediate the situation by that point. It was very clear he wanted me back in the team.'

Still, it was a tricky time for McAnuff.

'From a football point of view, it was absolutely sort of the lowest point of my career. I'm now sat in League Two, not even being able to play on a Saturday, training with the reserves and the kids. It was tough, but everyone else at the club, apart from the ownership group, was brilliant. I'd make sure I'm trying to help the kids. I can't do anything with the first team, but [I could] go in and try and offer a little bit of guidance, experience, and just try to be a positive influence as much as I can. I think they appreciated that. It was just a matter of getting my head down and hoping the situation would change a little bit.'

Unfortunately, nothing was changing anytime soon. Not for McAnuff, and not for the rest of the staff.

Assistant manager Andy Hessenthaler explains how Becchetti and his entourage would just turn up at the training ground en masse, questioning players and staff, asking who was playing at the weekend, probing the manager's choices. Every interaction undermining Hendon and his coaching staff further. At times, Becchetti could be found literally pointing at the board where the weekend's team had been written, pointing at names, saying 'he doesn't play' or 'no, he doesn't play there'. Hendon stood his ground as much as he could, but as Hessenthaler explained a few years later, 'It was too much unrest ... there were too many disruptions. It affected everything in the end.'

As the season progressed, the interference continued. And then Francesco Becchetti decided to take things further.

It was one the most extraordinary incidents of his regime.

The deepest darkest woods

'It sounds crackers,' said Hartlepool United manager Ronnie Moore, speaking to the *Hartlepool Mail*. He summed it up perfectly.

On Sunday 15 November, Orient lost 3-1 away at Hartlepool. Although still sitting in the play-off places after their romping start to the season, the team were on a run of only one win in 12 matches. Francesco Becchetti was not happy.

As the team travelled back on the 250-mile journey from Hartlepool by coach, Becchetti spoke to Ian Hendon. He informed his manager that the players would not be going home to their families that evening. Instead, the entire squad, non-playing staff included, were to go straight to the Marriott Hotel in Waltham Abbey. They were to spend the week there before their home match against York City the following Saturday.

The press picked up on the story, the *Daily Mail* declaring it a 'bizarre attempt to halt Orient's dramatic slump'. Matt Simpson recalls Ian Hendon being interviewed by Sky Sports, the manager trying to put on a brave face and toe the party line.

'The look in his face of despair was a picture. It's just like, "The chairman suggested it, and I thought, 'Why not? This

CHAPTER 5

is a great idea'.'" Matt is incredulous. 'You didn't think that!' he says. 'You thought it was a terrible idea!'

Players went to training at their Chigwell training ground five minutes from the hotel and were allowed to pop out and see their family, but for the entire week, they lived in the Marriott.

'So many things like that were happening,' continues Matt. 'It was just like, "Oh, of course they're all locked in a hotel for a week. What else would you expect?" I mean, you became a bit desensitised to it.'

To his credit, Hendon maintained his cool, telling the *Daily Mail*, 'The owner has had different sporting ventures over the years and he said sometimes it's good to get together and spend time together. It helps team bonding. When the owner suggested it, I thought why not try something different? If we win four or five-nil the owner might ask us to move here permanently. We're not trying to hide anything. We're staying at a hotel. There are plenty of army camps I know about in deepest darkest woods if we wanted to do that.'

For Paul Levy, it was clear that Hendon was doing his best to maintain a sense of normality under exceptionally difficult conditions.

'I think the more you look at it, and the more you listen to what was said at the time, the more you can really read into what was going on and what he was having to deal with. From that perspective, I admire him.'

Still, like the rest of the fanbase, Paul remembers feeling appalled by the situation.

'How can you treat people that way? How can you make people that have got families, that have children waiting for them at home – how can you lock them up and force them to go into a hotel for any period of time? Never mind a week. For what? What was the rationale behind? What do you think is going to be achieved from doing that? It made us a bit of a laughing stock.'

Laughing stock or not, on the following Saturday, Orient beat York at home. Despite everything, the team were heading towards December still in the play-off places and only five points off automatic promotion.

Becchetti had made his point.

And then, on Boxing Day, he kicked his assistant manager up the arse.

A little bit of banter

'Well, it is Boxing Day to be fair.'

Speaking on Sky Sports News, assistant manager Andy Hessenthaler does his best to make a joke out of the indefensible. Francesco Becchetti, the club president, has just kicked him up the backside on the pitch at Brisbane Road. It was, as the news reader announces, 'an extraordinary incident'.

Since the week spent in the hotel in Waltham Abbey, and the subsequent 3-2 victory over York City, Orient have drawn their next four league games and crashed out of the FA Cup. However, the Boxing Day fixture at home ends in victory over Portsmouth. Ollie Palmer bags two goals and Jay Simpson converts a penalty for the Os. Even Jobi McAnuff makes it into the team, boosting the midfield against a Portsmouth side pushing for promotion.

It is a great result. But it's not what anyone remembers.

The footage is there for everyone to see.

Hessenthaler walks on to the pitch in his tracksuit after the match. He sort of points at his ear, exchanging a word or two with someone. A second later, Becchetti, in a large green parka with a furry hood, marches on to the pitch in his blue jeans. He storms after his assistant manager, gesticulating by thrusting his arm out and touching his thumb to his

CHAPTER 5

index and middle fingers, shaking them in what can only be described as a 'stereotypical Italian' gesture. He then breaks into a run for a step or two and kicks Hessenthaler up the arse. The black loafer off his right foot connects perfectly with Hessenthaler's tracksuited cheeks.

'It's nothing, it's fine,' said Hessenthaler at the time. 'It's just a little bit of banter, a bit of stuff that's been going on in the last few weeks between us and it probably looked worse than what it was.'

Speaking on *The Circus Upstairs* a decade later, Hessenthaler confirms what everyone knew at the time.

'It was obviously played down by myself, but I think people know it wasn't banter, don't they?'

The FA knew. They handed Becchetti a six-match stadium ban and fined him £40,000 for violent conduct.

For the fans, it was just another example of Becchetti's farcical behaviour.

'Absolute clowns all over the shop,' says Paul Levy, reflecting on the incident. Like everyone else, he has no doubt that the president's actions were 'not a bit of banter'.

'You could see that absolutely wasn't the case whatsoever. I mean, at this level, people have very realistic income levels. And I say realistic by comparison to the Championship and the Premier League. They *need* jobs. They've got to put food on the table. They've got mortgages like we all have. They're not swanning around in luxurious cars and living in luxurious properties. So, I guess for Andy, he just wanted to toe the line. But quite frankly, I'm sure there was an employment tribunal to be had off the back of that situation.'

The aftermath of the incident was played out on Sky Sports. It shows Becchetti skipping around the side of the pitch, wearing his Orient shirt, slapping hands with fans. It's a bizarre dance for attention.

'He did a sort of lap of honour,' remembers Matt Simpson. 'He was going right up to all the fans and getting high fives. It was ridiculous. I was like, "Mate, you've relegated us six months ago. There is nothing for you to be celebrating." He was desperate for adoration. He's like a small child. He just wanted the glory. He wanted people to chant his name. He wanted everyone to look at him as the saviour of Orient. And he did the opposite.'

Becchetti's behaviour that day epitomised everything that was wrong with his ownership. As Matt explains, 'He failed terribly in actually managing the football club. He didn't understand what owning a football club or owning Leyton Orient actually entailed, because a club is so much more than the first team playing matches and winning or losing. A club is a community and a history and a collection of shared experiences. It has a dynamic of its own. He didn't understand any of that. He was an embarrassment.'

Embarrassing and ridiculous. 'Absolute clowns.' But ultimately, as Dave Victor says, all these incidents were 'sideshows'.

Becchetti's next moves threatened the very existence of the club.

6

'I don't really want to be a part of all this. Whatever you're offering me it's just not worth it. It's been two years where it's just been a shambles. As much as I love the club, I just couldn't carry on. Every day going to training, and thinking, "What's going to happen today?"'

> Club captain Mathieu Baudry, speaking to *The Circus Upstairs* on his last days at Leyton Orient.

After a 3-1 home defeat to Exeter in January 2016, Ian Hendon is sacked. Leyton Orient have only won four matches since September.

Becchetti appoints former Bolton, Newcastle and West Ham striker Kevin Nolan as player-manager. He lasts until April, when he is relieved of his duties as a manager. He is demoted to simply: player.

Assistant manager Andy Hessenthaler is appointed as caretaker manager for the last five games of the 2015/16 season, guiding the team to an eighth-placed finish, six points off the play-off positions.

Sixteen players, including Mathieu Baudry, Jobi McAnuff and Dean Cox leave the club in the summer. Cox, a hero of the 2014 play-off season, is forced out on transfer deadline day, unable to sign for another club until January 2017.

Leyton Orient start the 2016/17 season with Hessenthaler as manager.

By the end of October they are in the relegation zone, second from bottom.

Rumours of skulduggery

The Birkbeck Tavern is behind Leyton tube station, just round back of the High Street. In recent seasons it's been used as the designated pub for away fans on matchdays.

Back in November 2016, it was the site of a heated meeting of Leyton Orient supporters, all increasingly worried about their club.

Tom Davies was there. As the vice-chairman of LOFT, the Leyton Orient Fans' Trust, he was sitting behind a wooden table in an upstairs room, trying to hold the membership to order.

A member since the LOFT was first established in 2001, Davies soon found himself sitting on the committee. Their aim was and is simple: to provide an independent voice for Orient fans, keeping the club in check and making sure that fan voices are heard. With the club under the stewardship of Barry Hearn, a regular at LOFT's meetings, they hadn't had to do much.

'We sort of toddled on doing various little community initiatives,' Davies says. 'Having meetings with the club, trying to do a little bit here and there. We had a membership which was functional, but it was quite small. And obviously, when things started to get drastic, membership mushroomed.'

A sports journalist, working for *The Guardian* and *The Independent*, Davies had seen crisis-hit clubs before.

CHAPTER 6

'I did the conventional journalistic route of doing local papers, papers in London, papers in Leeds, then freelancing all over the place for a bit. I worked on the Enfield local paper when their ground was sold in the late 90s, and there was quite a lot of skulduggery going on there. Those sorts of stories have followed me around a bit.'

With increasing rumours of 'skullduggery' in east London, Davies and his fellow committee members found themselves meeting more regularly before the 2016/17 season kicked off. The 'sideshows' of the previous season were giving way to much deeper problems.

'The symbolism of Dean Cox leaving on transfer deadline day is a real turning point,' explains Davies. 'We had a task on our hands, and we had to step up, because we were being driven into the wall. There were a couple of lively meetings in the summer of 2016 where there was a sense of, "What's going on?" And all that bravado he [Becchetti] did, waving his scarf around and running on the pitch and kicking Andy Hesenthaler up the arse ... You realise then that that was all just posturing. It was obvious we were heading for a very bad place.'

The November crisis meeting was scheduled for a Thursday night in an upstairs room designed to accommodate 120 people. LOFT had met at the Birkbeck many times before, but that night was different. Over the past few weeks membership had doubled. Everyone wanted their say.

'That meeting at the Birkbeck was quite incredible,' says Davies. 'Quite often when we'd use that pub for our meetings, you could have the tables out and your pints on the tables. But this was people queueing down the stairs! You couldn't even peer around the corner and see who was in. It was absolutely rammed.'

Even the national press were on hand to document the occasion. David Hytner, writing in *The Guardian* at the time, summed up the panic of the gathered Orient fans, 'From their little corner of the capital, they fear that nobody is aware of their crisis and, if they are, they are not listening.'

Davies was doing his best to listen. But it wasn't an easy meeting to chair.

'There was a lot of passion and energy in the room. And sometimes people disagree with each other in quite a passionate, energetic way. We had to say, "So, what are we going to do here? Who's got the suggestion? What's the next step?" And it was trying to make sure you had the formal stuff to give yourself a mandate to do something else, vote on it properly, all that kind of democratic stuff. It's exhausting.'

LOFT were looking to make a stand at the next home game on the following Saturday, when Orient were due to host Blackpool. Coincidentally, Blackpool's fans' trust were also concerned about their own club's ownership. The timing made sense.

'We'd been in touch with Blackpool's fans' trust in the build up to that meeting,' says Davies. 'They were having a very similar sort of experience. So, we thought, "Well, we were playing them in late November, let's do a joint protest that day."'

The following Saturday, the two sets of supporters marched from the Birkbeck Tavern to Brisbane Road. Their messages the same, 'We want our club back.'

'There was some dissent,' remembers Davies. 'A couple of people sort of poured scorn on us as we walked past the supporters' club, stuff like that. You're always going to get a few who don't agree with you. But it was still the first step of something that was only going to grow with the current state of the club.'

The protest was the start of a fan-led movement. The game, a 2-1 defeat for Orient, marked a turning point in the relationship between fans and owner. From that moment on,

CHAPTER 6

Becchetti stopped attending matches. Davies's work was only just starting. He began organising more meetings, speaking to the press and preparing for the worst.

'It was exhausting,' he says. 'There were some long nights, and I spent a lot of time just chewing it over. Your mental energy is going on it quite a lot. But these things can be energising as well. Once you get the bit between your teeth, you can do it. But I don't recall having much time to do anything else or pursuing any other hobbies in great depth.'

Beyond the protest, the meeting cemented some of the thinking that many people had been wrestling with: what was the club's future?

'We started to talk about maybe down the line ... we might have to do fundraising,' explains Davies. 'And think about some kind of recovery fund or alternative contingency plan if the whole club went under. We were all really worried about that.'

As the season drifted on, the possibility of the club going under became a real possibility.

And then, in the spring, Leyton Orient were issued with a winding-up order.

It took just seven minutes
Monday, 20 March 2017, The Royal Courts of Justice
HMRC vs. Leyton Orient

Sometimes, football isn't about the football.

By March 2017, Leyton Orient were on to their fourth manager of the season. Andy Hessenthaler had lasted until October, making way for former Sampdoria boss Alberto Cavasin. An Italian who spoke very little English, communication was once again a problem. He was in charge for ten games. Future England under-20s coach Andy Edwards took over for a couple of months, before first-team coach Danny Webb took on the job, overseeing a team of largely youth team players competing in a league of seasoned professionals. Many first-team players had downed tools, been frozen out or been moved on. As Webb told the BBC after defeat to Stevenage in January, his team were made up of, 'Seventeen-, 18-year-olds. I do urge the fans, as frustrating as it is, to try and look to the future.'

But what future?

LOFT were increasingly worried. After the November meeting they released a statement 'calling for Becchetti to either commit to changing the way he runs the club, or to put the club up for sale'. Becchetti did neither. He simply withdrew, no longer attending matches, refusing to engage with shareholders or supporters. As ever, supporters, players, staff and managers were left wondering what was going on.

At the start of 2017, chief executive Alessandro Angelieri issued a statement in defence of Becchetti, claiming that the squad he inherited, the squad a penalty away from the Championship, was 'a squad without future'. He also claimed, 'Mr Becchetti has a great charisma and the players definitely feel his absence.'

It was another bizarre statement, but maybe there was a glint of light in the darkness. A commitment that Becchetti would carry on funding the club 'within common sense' as well as a consideration to sell the club if 'appropriate offers' were forthcoming.

The problem was, Leyton Orient were no longer a particularly attractive prospect. The club had lost £4.4m in Becchetti's first season alone. It now had outstanding debts of £9m.

After a defeat to top-of-the-table Doncaster at Brisbane Road, with former Orient captain Mat Baudry scoring the fourth goal of the game for his new club, Leyton Orient sat bottom of League Two. It was their 16th home defeat of the season. Relegation out of the Football League was a near certainty.

It was the least of the club's worries.

In March, club staff were forced to shout for help, issuing statements on social media. Staff, like the players, hadn't received their monthly wages. There was widespread sympathy, but the authorities, and Becchetti, did nothing. It appeared he was no longer funding the club.

On the Monday after the Doncaster defeat, Leyton Orient Football Club Limited was in court. At the start of March, Her Majesty's Revenue and Customs served the club with a winding-up petition on the grounds of unpaid tax. Reportedly for a sum of £250,000, the case could have seen the club fall into liquidation.

In the end, the hearing took just seven minutes. Becchetti settled the tax bill, his lawyers stating that he intended to commit another £1m to the club over the next couple of months. There was a stay of execution, and the case was adjourned until June.

Leyton Orient would not be liquidated or placed into administration. Yet. But the uncertainty and chaos remained. Not only were Orient still likely to be relegated out of the Football League for the first time in 112 years, but staff at the club were still not being paid.

Staff like Ada Martin.

'Oh, Harri's gone'

'I find it a difficult thing to talk about it,' says Ada, as we talk in a hospitality room overlooking the pitch at Brisbane Road. 'It wasn't just a job to me. It was my club at the same time.'

Back in April 2016, Ada had made a stand. 'I just lost my head,' he says.

The kit manager since 2008, he's been working at the club since 1994 when his dad asked the groundsman if there was anything his boy could do. 'He ain't doing a lot now since he left school,' Ada recalls his father saying. Eventually he took over the head groundsman position but was forced into a different role when he suddenly found himself recovering from the effects of a car crash.

'I got back ended by a van,' he says. 'Then I found out, while I was at home with my feet up, that the kit man was leaving. I said, "I'm not doing nothing at the moment, put my name forward."' He interviewed for the job and was given the role. Ada has been Leyton Orient's kit manager ever since; a constant presence in an otherwise ever-evolving changing room.

Another constant presence at the club is Ada's wife, club secretary Lindsey Martin.

'She started after me,' Ada explains. 'She's done over 23 years now. Started off as a steward. And then she came in to help out. They needed some extra help in the ticket office and her role developed from that.'

Two stalwarts of the club, who met at work (Lindsey's work at Orient would later be honoured by the EFL with the Club Employee Award at their annual award ceremony in 2024), theirs is a marriage both emotionally and fiscally attached to Leyton Orient. If anyone was going to stand up to Becchetti and his team, it was Ada.

In April 2016, the day after Kevin Nolan was relieved of his managerial duties and asked to remain as a player, Becchetti made another change. Lee Harrison, the club's well-respected and well-liked goalkeeping coach, was sacked. He was replaced in that role by the head of recruitment, Roberto Gagliardi. It was another bizarre decision in the never-ending list of bizarre decisions.

'Every day within the training ground, you didn't know what was going to happen,' says Ada. 'This day, I walked in and they said, "Oh, Harri's [Lee Harrison] gone. They

CHAPTER 6

don't want him no more. Gagliardi is coming back in as goalkeeping coach." I went, "Oh, this is a joke. Someone's got to make a stand. Why don't we all just pack it in?" Spur-of-the-moment stuff but treating Harri like that was wrong.'

A staff meeting was called. Chief executive Alessandro Angelieri, alongside COO Vito Miceli, addressed the footballing staff and informed them that Becchetti had made his decisions. Lee Harrison was going, Kevin Nolan was now a player, Andy Hessenthaler was stepping up to be manager and Gagliardi was the team's new goalkeeping coach.

'I went, "You're a joke,"' says Ada. 'I pointed to Kevin Nolan. "What do you think? He's going to play for you? He won't play. He's just been the manager."'

He then pointed at Lee Harrison.

'"And you get rid of him. For this bloke [indicating Gagliardi]. You're a shambles." Gagliardi played in goal once, and they thought he could coach as well at the same time. I said, "You're all a joke. You can't even answer me." I just walked out.'

The following day, Ada arrived back at the training ground. Becchetti had been there. He had called another meeting. Ada was one of the main subjects of conversation.

'He got them all into the canteen again and was praising me. He goes, "Why can't you show passion like the kit man?" He thought if you show passion like the kit man, maybe we'll be winning more games.

'If people lose their jobs in life, and if they deserve it, then fine. But if you're losing your job for no reason, it don't sit right with me. Don't sit right. And it didn't with Harri, because he's such a lovely geezer.'

A year later, Ada wasn't just standing up for his colleagues. As Becchetti began to withdraw the funds that were necessary to the running of the club, Ada had no choice but to stand up for himself and his wife as well. Waking up on pay day in March 2017, the Martins discovered that neither of them had been paid.

'It didn't surprise a lot of us at the time. They were late once with the money because they couldn't get the funds over from Italy. In those days, you accepted it. But when we didn't get paid this time, it felt different. No one said anything. We just woke up that morning and there was no money in there.'

It was left to Vito Miceli to attempt to allay club staff's fears.

'You give it a week, don't you?' says Ada. 'You don't throw the towel in. And we had a meeting at the training ground. They're giving you a lot of bullshit about our money. So, you might as well hit them the whole time: "Why aren't you going to pay us? When are you going to pay us?"

'It went on to month two, same meeting. "You will get paid, the president's having trouble transferring money." The same thing. And after the second month, the players get their money from the PFA. But the staff didn't. I think it was month three by the time we got paid.'

I ask Ada how he was feeling at the time. Was he anxious for himself and Lindsey?

'I was more worried about the club,' he explains. 'Whether the club would survive. I got offered two or three jobs at that time from other clubs. I would have been OK. The missus would have been OK. But you're more worried about the club surviving. They're talking about applying to the Essex Senior League! And that was the reality of it. We did come very, very, very close to actually not existing any more, because he [Becchetti] pulled all his money out.

'The only money coming in the club was on the matchday. They'd cash all that up. None of it would be banked. It'd just be used to run the club for the next couple of weeks. We went to Crewe as an overnighter. We lost 3-0 and we paid for the hotel with pound coins from the takings of the last game!

CHAPTER 6

The bank accounts were shut. The credit card was maxed out. That's just what it was like.'

More than ever, it was the staff and the fans who were keeping the club together. Staff like Ada.

Fans like Keren Harrison.

Getting the badge in

You don't have to work for a football club for it to be your life. Like Ada, Keren Harrison has put the hours in. And so have her family.

'I wasn't going to let having kids stop me going to football,' she says. 'Rhiannon came to her first game at 11 days old and Nathan came to his first game at seven days old. He was born Christmas Eve. I wasn't allowed to take him to the Boxing Day game.'

Everyone knows Keren. She's at every match, home and away. She's the membership secretary at the supporters' club. For nearly a decade she was the supporter liaison officer. When Matt Porter was ousted by Becchetti, Keren stepped up. She did what she could to get supporters' voices heard by the Italians. 'They did listen to a certain degree,' she says. 'Whether they actually did anything is another matter.'

We're sitting in a nice cafe (Prestige Awards, Boutique Cafe of the Year 2021/22 no less) for coffee and a peppermint tea on the new side of Harlow. Keren arrives in her Leyton Orient hoodie. She always gets the badge in.

'Little fun fact,' she says. 'My cousin co-designed the Orient badge. There was a competition back in the 1970s or 80s or something.'

For Keren, Orient runs about as deep as it can. It's always been a part of her family.

'My mum was a golden girl in the 60s – a half-time, 50-50 ticket seller. She's been going 70-plus years.'

Born in one of the terraced houses of Dunedin Road on the other side of Coronation Gardens next to Brisbane Road, Keren's mum, Rose, started attending Orient matches in the 1950s. When Keren and her siblings came along, they'd visit their grandparents next to the ground, taking it in turns to go and watch matches.

'Mum and Dad couldn't afford to take us all. But we all used to go around and stand in the back garden knowing when there was a goal. When I first started working and got my own money the first thing I did was I bought a season ticket on the North Terrace. In front of the men's toilets. I used to stand there with my dad and mum and a little group of friends that mum and dad had made.

'When I started dating my now husband, I said to him, "If you want to see me on a Saturday, I'm at Orient. If not, I'll see you whenever." Which is apparently what my mum said to my dad back in the late 60s. So, he started coming over the Orient as well.'

The entire family still sit together – Keren, her mum, her sister, her two children and her husband, Mark. Mark now has a very important job on matchdays. He prepares the beers for the supporters' club.

'It takes over his life more than everything that I do with Orient takes over my life,' says Keren. 'Can't get away from it. It's in both of our lives so deep that we arrange holidays around it. We turn down family functions because of it. And that's why, whenever there's a cup draw, we always pray for an away game so that we can enjoy it ourselves.'

As the club drifted into the last six weeks of the 2016/17 season, nobody was enjoying themselves. In April, the club doctor resigned. Like the rest of the staff, he hadn't been paid for months. In the background, LOFT were actively raising funds to protect the future of the club, setting out ambitious plans to raise £100,000. They were also in active talks with other fans' trusts and investigating the possibility of a phoenix club – setting up a new club to continue the Orient name should Leyton Orient die. It was a last resort, but it was seriously being considered.

I ask Keren how she felt, contemplating the fact that Orient might not exist for much longer.

'Awful,' she says. 'It's such a big part of my life. I was thinking, "Well, if we've got no supporters' club, what do I do on a Saturday?" How do I explain to the kids that we've gone bust? Somebody's come in and taken all the money and run away. How do you explain that to a seven- and a nine-year-old?'

For every Keren who goes home and away with her family, there's many more who will rarely go to an away match but will be sat in their seat next to the same people at every home game. There's the fan who goes once a month with their daughter or their uncle or their best friend. There's someone who goes every New Year's Day with their old mates from school. It's an annual catch-up, they have a beer and they watch the Os. There's someone who makes sure they check the Orient score on a Saturday afternoon because their grandad used to be a season ticket holder. There's someone who once went to Brisbane Road with an old work colleague and wants to go again when they have a bit more time.

There are thousands of someones, all with a different relationship with the club, all with a different level of Orient passion. They all have the club in their life. It's part of their identity.

They were about to lose a piece of themselves.

An impossible task

While Orient's fans fretted about the future of the club, the club's remaining players were left fighting for survival in the Football League.

The latest manager, Danny Webb, resigned at the end of March. Speaking after a fourth straight defeat, away at Crawley Town a few days before, talkSPORT reported Webb as saying, 'We are all in limbo. I am out of contract at the end of the season and the frustrating thing is I am trying to think ahead and think about the future when I am not guaranteed a future.' Soon afterwards, the club confirmed his resignation.

The task of leading Leyton Orient's young squad through the final seven games of the season fell to assistant manager Omer Riza.

'He is very determined to make sure that the team finishes the season strong and he's looking forward for the challenge,' came a statement from the club.

It was an impossible task. Riza was not offered a pay rise for his new managerial duties. In fact, like the rest of the staff, he wasn't even being paid.

Speaking to the Leyton Orient fan podcast *The LO Down* a few years later, Riza explained the situation.

'It was crazy. I didn't know what squad or what team I had. One thing I did know is that the youngsters were there. They would do exactly what I asked of them, they would work hard. And then there were some pros, Micky Collins, Liam Kelly, Callum Kennedy ... there were players who would put their heart on their sleeves. It was tough, in respect of not being able to plan. I planned as best we could.'

Two defeats in a row put Orient on the brink of relegation, but Riza and the team continued to fight.

'It was ... let's get through these two months,' he continued. 'Let's make sure the club don't pick up this problem, [or] that problem, get the players through to the end of the season. None of us were being paid.'

Slim hopes of avoiding relegation were fuelled by a 2-2 draw away at promotion chasing Luton Town, before a battling victory at home to relegation rivals Hartlepool over Easter. The kids were fighting until the end.

Paul Levy, like many fans, had sympathy with the players, both the first team and their young replacements.

'You could see some of them were putting in a shift,' he says. 'And the younger, inexperienced players were really quite well supported. It wasn't their fault that we were losing games. We were playing the youth team because some of the players refused to play. At the time, I was like, "Well, maybe they should have carried on playing," but quite rightly [they didn't]. You're being badly treated. You're not being given a work environment to excel in. You're not being paid. You're probably the main breadwinner in your household. Why would you? I get it. They don't have the affinity to the club like we do. For them, it's their career.'

With three games left, Orient could still mathematically escape. They would need to win every match and hope Hartlepool failed to pick up two more points.

By the end of 2016/17 Orient had fewer wins in the season than they had managers since Becchetti took over. Including interim appointments and Kevin Nolan as player-manager, a total of 11 men had served under the president.

Omer Riza was the last manager Becchetti would appoint.

He looked like he might be the last manager Leyton Orient ever had.

7

Saturday 22 April 2017. Orient are playing away at Crewe Alexandra.

The match kicks off at Gresty Road at 3pm. By half-time it is all over. Three first-half goals put Crewe 3-0 up, securing their league safety and condemning the Os to relegation. Other results ensure Orient will finish at the very bottom of the EFL's 92 teams.

The BBC report from the match is damning, 'This campaign represents a new low for one of the English Football League's oldest clubs. As well as the ongoing managerial uncertainty, Orient are in "mortal danger" of going out of business, according to the legal adviser to their fans' trust. Owner Francesco Becchetti has been given until 12 June to pay off debts or sell the club. Staff have still not been paid their March wages, and club employees have said they are "hugely concerned" by a lack of communication from the Orient hierarchy. Results on the pitch have been poor throughout the season, with the club having both the worst attacking and worst defensive record in the division. Relegation was staved off for one more week with victory over Hartlepool on Easter Monday, but their 28th defeat of the season leaves them facing a dubious future in the National League.'

CHAPTER 7

'Sixty-fucking-three-years!'
Saturday, 29 April 2017, Brisbane Road
Leyton Orient 1 Colchester United 3

There's only so much you can do as a supporter.

A week after relegation is confirmed, the fanbase make their biggest move. On Easter Monday, after the victory over Hartlepool (the team's first victory in months), there had been a post-match protest. People dressed up as clowns, people blew whistles. But this feels different. This feels angry. This feels big.

Colchester United are the opponents. Three years earlier, this fixture saw Russell Slade receive his infamous ultimatum from the new owner after a 2-0 home defeat. For many, that marked the real start of the Becchetti regime. At the time, Orient fans were fearing for the future. Now their worst nightmares have come true.

Orient are 3-0 down after 85 minutes and there's a febrile atmosphere in the stands.

There's a larger police presence than normal. Trouble is not unexpected. 'Becchetti out! Becchetti out!' rings out from the home fans. You can hear the pain in the voices. It's spat with passion.

A flare flies through the air, launched from the South Stand. It lands in the middle of the Colchester United penalty box. Red smoke drifts back towards the goal, filling the stand behind it. At that moment the first protesters start running on to the pitch. They are young, bouncing. They look like kids. Seconds later a handful of the older lads start to join them. Men, not boys. They're angry, defiant.

In the corner of the South Stand, where it joins the main West Stand, the police presence suddenly looks small. They're attempting to hold back the older lads who are filtering through. One man is marched out of the ground.

There's an older man, grey hair, late 60s, maybe in his 70s, doing a Brian Clough impression. He's clipping people round the ear as they run past him on to the pitch. Trying to hold back the pitch invaders. He swings a punch at one who avoids it and makes his way past him. You don't enter the field of play. It's now his mission to stop anyone getting on the pitch, whatever the legitimacy of the protest.

People are running on to the pitch from all sides of the ground now. There are far more fans than players on the grass, so the referee calls it, ordering the teams down the tunnel. Orient players understand what's happening. A few tap supporters on the back as they pass. This has been coming.

A minute later, and the flow of fans is overwhelming. This is a full pitch invasion. A couple of the older gents have seen enough, they don't want to get involved and make their way to the exit, but most are still in the stands, seeing what unfolds. Many are also on the pitch. The Brian Clough impersonator is still having a pop.

'I've been coming here 63 years. Sixty-fucking-three years,' he rages at a young fan who's answered back, trying to explain why this protest is justified.

On the pitch, 'I'm Orient 'till I die' is sung in one voice. The club might die before the fans do. It's every football supporter's greatest fear.

Paul Levy is sat in the South Stand with his fellow podcast host, Steve Nussbaum. The red flare is still burning in the penalty box in front of him. Like many others, he's not sure what to do. Invading the pitch is something you simply don't do in the middle of a game. It's ingrained into you ever since you start going to football. There are signs on the inside of the advertising hoardings, facing the stands, telling you to keep off the playing surface. The only time you ever go on is to celebrate if your team is lucky enough

CHAPTER 7

to win the league or get promoted. Once in a decade (less if you're Orient) supporters might go on to celebrate victory in a massive cup game. It's always in good spirits. Never in anger.

'At first, I was a little bit like, "Oh, what do we do here?" says Paul. "Should I, shouldn't I? Should we, shouldn't we?" Steve and I stayed in our seats for quite a few minutes.'

Lots of supporters are still doing the same. But it's not just kids and lads on the pitch. This isn't just a small section of the fanbase.

'We saw old people walking on the pitch, so we thought, "You know what? Let's go and join this protest."'

Chants of 'Fuck the EFL' are ringing out around the ground. Everyone knows it's not solely Becchetti's fault. Why was this allowed to happen in the first place? Football clubs aren't simply a business to be sold for the highest price. They need protecting. They're part of the people. Part of the community. They aren't there to make money. Not for the fans, rarely for the owners. They make money for the leagues and the governing bodies. For the people in charge only. Fuck the EFL.

On the pitch, Paul turns to look at the Colchester fans. They're joining in with the chants. Their east London rivals down the A12 are in danger of extinction. This fixture, this club – it's a part of their lives too. They have friends and family who support Leyton Orient. They can empathise. This could easily be them.

'All credit to Colchester United who were very much on our side,' says Paul. 'They could have been very much not on our side given the rivalry ... But I think they put that to one side, and to their great credit supported us and chanted with us. For that, they will always have a piece of respect from me.'

Meanwhile, the protest is massing under the directors' box. The anger is rising.

Waiting for the Herberts

Lifelong fan Billy Herring is down the front. To his surprise, his dad is with him.

They'd arrived at the game as they always do. Billy's dad driving up from Essex. The same routine they've had for years. His dad took him to his first match when he was just 18 months old. 'I cried through the whole of the first half,' says Billy. 'That should have told him something.'

Despite the tearful start, they've been going together ever since.

Now in his early 40s, Billy still sits with his dad. Before the match, in their seats at the back of the West Stand, Billy prepped him on the plan.

'As happens on social media, we'd had the messages go around. "When the Herberts go to the corner, that's the signal." We all knew what was going to happen. I said to my old man, "Look, this is what's going to happen." And my old man went, "Oh, I'm too old for all that bollocks, Bill. I'm not getting on the pitch. I can barely get up the stairs, let alone get down!"'

His dad said he'd wait for him outside after the match and they sat back to watch the game. Billy was ready for the flare at 85 minutes. He wasn't ready for his dad's reaction.

'When the flare went on, my old man knocked me over to get on to the pitch! He literally pushed me out of the way to get past me. He just did it. Boom.' Billy followed.

Like many fans, this was the first time he had crossed that white line in anger. The only other time Billy had stepped on the playing surface was in celebration, six years earlier.

It's one of those nights that has gone down in Orient history. One of Barry Hearn's top ten sporting moments. The night in 2011 when Orient drew 1-1 with Arsenal in the fifth round of the FA Cup, substitute Jonathan Téhoué

CHAPTER 7

skipping through the Gunners' defence to score a stunning 89th-minute equaliser and earn Orient a replay at the Emirates.

The game had finished and the reporter from Sky Sports was on the grass, filming a handover back to the studio. The celebrating Orient fans were in the background, Billy among them.

'I just hopped over the barrier and put an Orient flag around his shoulders,' says Billy. 'The steward looked at me as I was about to go over. And I kind of looked at him as if to say, "Can I?" And he purposely looked the other way.'

The joy and optimism of 2011 feels a lifetime away for the Orient fans protesting on the pitch against Colchester in 2017. An announcement is made. The game has been abandoned.

'The real kick between the legs was when we were all told to clear the pitch,' says Paul Levy. 'The game was not going ahead. You can all go home. Then we really learned what the EFL were about.'

Almost two hours after the protest started, the game is restarted, the final eight minutes being played behind closed doors. Paul, like many fans, still feels betrayed by the EFL's actions throughout the Becchetti reign. He understands that for the integrity of the game, that particular match needed to be finished. But the general lack of concern for Orient's grievances was reinforced by the deception in the Football League's statement.

'A decision was taken with the police to announce that the game had been abandoned, as it was felt this would help clear the pitch, which proved correct,' it read. 'However, it was deemed appropriate that the game needed to be played to a conclusion in order to maintain the integrity of the competition and in respect of Colchester United's position of being able to qualify for the League Two play-offs.'

It wasn't as if this protest was a surprise. Orient had been fighting for survival for months. The perception was that the EFL had been doing little, if nothing, to help.

'I don't really know what else we could have done,' says Billy. 'We were left with no alternative. We tried everything else. We tried peaceful negotiations with the club. We tried to get in contact with the club. There were lots of people doing lots of good work in the background, trying to work and mediate. They didn't want to know. Ultimately, you push people to a certain point, they're going to break, and they're going to react.'

Billy, like Paul, had been fighting for his team for weeks. Fighting for his club wherever he went.

In fact, he nearly had a fight with Francesco Becchetti.

It's not only a game

Before the Leyton Orient president almost hit him, Billy had been wearing his 'Becchetti Out' shirt all around town.

'I took that shirt to the London Marathon, because we were watching our mate run round,' he says. 'Every time there was a camera, I held up the shirt. I wanted to get it on TV.'

His best mate being an Arsenal fan, he also found himself invited to the FA Cup semi-final that same day: Arsenal vs. Manchester City at Wembley.

'We were right down the front, and I was just holding the shirt up the whole time. All these Arsenal fans we were sat with were like, "What the fuck is all that?" And I remember going into the pub [after the game, which Arsenal had won 2-1] with my best mate, and he was like, "Mate, for fuck's sake. Put that shirt away." And I was like, "Nah, bollocks." We got chatting to these Arsenal fans, and I got the whole of the Arsenal pub singing "Becchetti out! Becchetti out!" And it was brilliant. It was their day, and I made it about the Orient. I had had a few beers.'

CHAPTER 7

Luckily, Billy was sober a few weeks earlier when the Leyton Orient owner noticed his recently made T-shirt. 'I was standing by the side of the pitch,' he says. 'Holding the shirt up to the players. I see Becchetti on the sidelines by the dugout. I turned around and I showed it to him. And in the same way, when he ran on the pitch and kicked Andy Hessenthaler up the arse, he started marching towards me. And when I say marching, he had a *proper* march on. One of his minders or someone put their hand on his shoulder to stop him and just said, "No, no, no, no." And I remember him [Becchetti] looking at me. He would have come over. He *would* have come over. If it was down to him. He was on his way.'

An actor, writer and respected former teacher, Billy is not prone to outbursts of violence. But provoking Francesco Becchetti was different.

'I'm five-foot-six and I'm not a troublemaker, but it was one of them where you just go, "Go on. Give me an excuse. I'll let you have the first one." And I know this sounds so petty, but it was a small victory.'

For fans like Billy, Keren Harrison and Paul Levy, the fact that their club had been torn apart was heartbreaking. The fact that it might no longer exist meant they had to contemplate the possibility they might lose something they love. I ask Billy what he was thinking during those dark days. What would he do if the worst did happen, and Leyton Orient died?

'I said I'd never watch football again. If the FA had let the Os go bust, I would never have watched another game of football, ever again. I played football since I was seven years old. I played semi-pro when I was at uni. I played all the way through. It's been a massive part of my life. But I said I'd never watch another game again, ever. Nothing. I wouldn't entertain it at all.'

For some people who don't follow football, it's easy to dismiss the love fans have for their club. But for many it's a constant in your life for decades. It's just as real as any other type of affection.

'I remember when we went to the court and they basically gave the last extension,' explains Billy. 'I remember sitting with my wife, and I was just reading about it on the news. I just had tears running down my eyes, and she was like, "What is wrong with you?" I was like, "I'm going to lose the Os." And she said the infamous words, "It's only a game." I was like, "You don't understand what it means."'

But what does it mean?

'It's been in my family my whole life,' says Billy. 'My granddad went, my uncle goes, my dad goes. It's always been in our family. I suppose, to me, it is about family. You know? My godfather goes to the Os and sits with us as well. And he disappeared for about ten years or so. Then just one day, out of the blue, he turned up again. It was like he'd never been missing.'

Billy's Orient family is categorised by more than just blood ties. Theirs, like many others, is a group who've been sitting together for years. And just like with your real family, you care how they get on. The club is the place you meet every other week to catch-up with your friends and family, watch the match and be part of something bigger than just yourself. It's a lifelong commitment.

'I try never to get too up with the results and too down with the results and stuff,' says Billy. 'But they've made me cry more times than anything else in my life. I remember when we got promoted in 1988/89, that was the last game my granddad ever went to. He had a stroke that night because the excitement of the game was too much for him. He had a stroke *that* evening. And that was the last game he went to. The Os is always in the background. It's always there.'

CHAPTER 7

In April 2017, Leyton Orient were not only relegated out of the Football League. They were on the brink of no longer existing.

A really, long, long, journey home
Saturday, 6 May 2017, Bloomfield Road

Blackpool 3 Leyton Orient 1

There was time for one more protest before the season finished.

On the final day of the season, relegated Leyton Orient made the 250-mile journey to Bloomfield Road to take on a Blackpool team pushing to secure a place in the play-offs. It was a comprehensive 3-1 defeat for the Os.

Paul Levy, like almost 1,000 other Orient fans, made the four-and-a-half-hour journey to support his team.

'I think that was probably rock bottom,' he says. 'I just remember it being a bit of a weird day. There were lots of fans that I'd sort of known through social media, people I'm getting to meet. So, on the one hand, it was eventful. It was joyous. But on the other hand, it was our last ever game in the Football League for the foreseeable future.'

The fact that Orient fans were there at all wasn't guaranteed. At the start of the week, Blackpool announced their decision that there would be no tickets available for away supporters. A statement from the club said their 'decision was taken following a number of concerns', one of those being the prospect of another pitch invasion from Orient supporters. It was a claim that LOFT fought with the authorities, petitioning the EFL to ensure that tickets were made available.

'There is nothing to suggest Leyton Orient's supporters will be anything but peaceful,' read the LOFT statement. 'The pitch invasion protest at their last home match was peaceful in nature, with no violence. There has been no suggestion by the police that public order offences took place, nor were there any arrests for such offences. Indeed, the protest saw protesters on crutches, in mobility scooters and with small children in tow. Leyton Orient and its supporters has no history of violent protest.'

In the end, the EFL reversed the decision, and no pitch invasion took place. Fans from both sides joined together in a pre-match protest against their respective owners, marching along Blackpool promenade to the ground.

It was a display of Orient unity that hadn't always been reflected over the previous three years. Becchetti's ownership was divisive as well as disruptive. It not only created chaos, it created division.

'I was one of the first people who was like, "Ah, I want him gone,"' says Billy Herring. 'I remember arguing with my mates about it. And I remember my mate saying to me when we got relegated back to League Two, "Look, sometimes when you buy a house, you have to gut it first, or you can't start improving it." And I thought, "Yeah, OK. Fair point."'

His opinion didn't change for long.

'I remember the very first protest, which was to go into the ground five minutes late. I remember when I walked into the ground, some of the lads we sit with turned around and went, "Oh, you weren't outside with that bunch of dickheads, were you?" There must have been about ten people outside. That was it. But I was like, "Yeah, I was. I absolutely was."'

Opinion on Becchetti continued to divide the fanbase all the way to the final few games of the season.

'There were some people who were sitting there who would not hear a bad word about Becchetti,' says Billy. 'Almost to the very, very, very end, they would defend him.'

Another protest saw people dressing up as clowns, reflecting the circus that had engulfed the club.

CHAPTER 7

'There was one guy,' he says. 'He came up and he kept blowing this whistle and it was getting really annoying. And my dad's mate, who was in his 60s, went to this guy, "Mate. Do you mind?" And the guy wearing this clown [costume] was like, "You say something to me again and I'm going to whack you!" Tensions were high with everyone.'

Keren Harrison stayed clear of the protests, but she still did her bit, raising money to pay club staff as much as she could.

'I didn't want to be seen to be antagonising, being a ringleader or whatever,' she tells me. 'But myself, my sister, a couple others from the committee – we joined up together with LOFT, went and shook our buckets and said, "Please help us." I remember doing it at Tottenham. I remember doing it at Luton. The thought of losing Leyton Orient ... it couldn't be real. Going out and shaking a bucket had a practical use. I felt like I was doing something to help the club, trying to keep the club alive. Otherwise, it'll be like I'd just stood back and let my club fail, and I'm not having that. I love it too much.'

Back in Blackpool, the Orient fans started their journey home.

Paul Levy was in a car with his mate. As they travelled south down the M6, he scrolled his social accounts. 'It just felt like a really long, long journey home' he says. 'I think we had talkSPORT on, and just watching all the tweets coming in, people's memories, people's thoughts; despair, shock, sadness, all these negative emotions that people had. And anger, some real anger towards the ownership of the club, at how it had been run so badly into the ground. Yeah, it was a long journey.'

A long journey, and a long time to think. Like everyone, Paul was very worried about the prospect of competing in the National League.

'Look at Wrexham,' he says. 'It took them 15 years to get back up. It's not an easy league to get out of. And there was nothing to be happy about. "Where do we go from here? Is this bastard still going to own our club?" Were we even going to have a club to support? My mentality was, "What's next. How do we move forwards?"'

It was the question every Leyton Orient fan was asking: what next?

8

'Becchetti never understood money or management. These guys understand both.'

Barry Hearn, December 2023

Cryptic Kent

On 15 June 2017, a man called Kent Teague posted a tweet.

'Being a leader is not being a controller. More of a balance between a King & a servant. Directing when needed. Clearing paths for others.'

If you stumbled across his profile, you'd see that Teague was an American businessman, a former Microsoft employee with a list of other tech companies to his name. His bio lists his previous employment alongside the description, 'Doing the accomplishment thing for a while.'

Over the following days and weeks, he continued to communicate in a series of no-context riddles, including, '"Success is the ability to go from one failure to another with no loss of enthusiasm" – Sir Winston Churchill.'

The more he posted, the more rumours spread.

'Short term some overspend & win in a year, but ours will be an example of winning consistently over long periods of time. Commitment is key.'

The more the Orient fanbase watched on. 'Sometimes the existence of an NDA is part of an NDA, thus making it where no one can mention the NDA exists. I've signed a few like this.'

Cryptic Kent was born.

Kingmaker

Looking back, Matt Porter knows that being sacked by Francesco Becchetti was for the best.

'Long-term, it was a benefit without a doubt. There was no point in me being there, because I couldn't do anything. And actually, it was a blessing in disguise. It gave me the opportunity to operate in the shadows.'

In November 2016, as Leyton Orient sat on the edge of the relegation zone, Porter sent an email to long-term club sponsor Nigel Travis, CEO of Dunkin' Donuts. Now in his 70s, Travis is a boyhood Orient fan. Born in South Woodford, three miles from Brisbane Road, he saw his first Orient game in 1959. He's been, in his own words, 'fanatical' ever since.

Porter had already spoken to Travis about the potential to step in as the new owner of Leyton Orient. On paper, he was the perfect person to save the club from Becchetti.

'He [Travis] was still coming over for games,' says Porter. 'And he had a good relationship with them [the owners] because he was still putting money into the club through sponsorship. And he carried on doing that to keep that relationship going.'

Porter remembers Travis saying, 'I don't want to own Leyton Orient, but I will save if I have to.' This time the severity of the situation was spelt out to him.

'The email said, "I know you said you don't want to own it, and you'll only do it if you have to save it. Well, now you need to save it." And then we started talking.'

If Porter hadn't been operating in the shadows, who knows what might have happened. He did as much as anyone to try and save Leyton Orient.

It's the reason Dave Victor describes him as 'The Kingmaker'.

But would Nigel Travis wear the crown?

CHAPTER 8

The man who would be king?

Nigel Travis always knew Becchetti was the wrong man for Leyton Orient.

It was the summer of the Italian's takeover, and the team were playing Ipswich in their final pre-season game at Brisbane Road. Travis took his two young children. As a sponsor he and his family had always been welcome to sit with the club directors. But things had changed.

'I took my two kids and he [Becchetti] refused, despite the fact I was a sponsor, to let them go in the directors' area. And then, because they were kids, he pushed them to the end of the balcony. I remember saying, "Wow, this is going to be different."

Like many associated with Leyton Orient, Travis still won't mention Becchetti's name. 'I can't say his name, because I'd have to put money in the tin,' he explains. In all his recollections, Becchetti is simply referred to as 'Mr B'.

A few weeks later, Travis went to speak to Mr B's chief executive, Alessandro Angelieri.

'I said, "Look, I want to be helpful. I'm a sponsor. Can I help you?" And Alessandro, who was a really nice guy, kept talking about the "president". I said, "For fuck's sake, stop talking about the president! He's someone who's invested in a football club." And I think that summed it up, because they just did whatever he did. And that's the opposite to me.'

As much as Travis is the opposite to Becchetti, he has plenty in common with former Orient chairman Barry Hearn. Both east London boys, two years apart in age, they even went to the same school. Yes, they are different personalities ('Barry is an out-and-out entrepreneur'), but maybe they both had something to prove.

'I was a pretty poor student at Buckhurst Hill County High School,' says Travis. 'And my wife found this report up in the loft one day, and it talked about me in about 1963 or

'64. It said I was "a very mediocre, a very average student". I wasn't very good. I felt inhibited because my voice didn't break until I was about 16 or 17. So that held me back. I had a squeaky voice. And then when it finally changed, I kind of used it a lot.'

He used it to good effect. His CV speaks for itself. Starting out in human resources, Travis was soon running companies and leading major businesses across Europe and the USA – from Blockbuster ('You could say I got out at the right time, but we were incredible. The year I left was the most successful year in Blockbuster history') and Papa Johns to Burger King and Dunkin' Donuts. He's the reason you can't stop at a motorway service station in the UK without seeing a Burger King.

'I've been very lucky, and I've always loved what I do,' he says. 'I have fun. And I try and create a fun environment.'

Of course, running businesses on either side of the Atlantic got in the way of being a match-going Orient fan on a regular basis.

'I stayed fervently Leyton Orient, but then life moved on. I moved to the States once, then twice and I didn't see Orient as much as I used to. In 1989 [when Orient beat Wrexham in the Fourth Division play-off final], I was in Miami for Burger King and the only way I got the Orient result was when my dad sent a fax! There was no other way of finding the results. There was no email. You couldn't listen to the game or watch it. I probably saw two games a year.'

Travis recalls seeing a match around Christmas in Becchetti's first season. 'I was appalled. I remember sitting next to Matt Porter and saying, "God, this is going to become awful. We're going to have to try and find a way to buy this club." And then nothing really happened.'

It wasn't until Porter's email in November 2016 that things started to move forward.

CHAPTER 8

'I heard that some guys who'd previously been at Derby were looking at a bid. I went to New York and met with these guys. We had a really good discussion. And we started doing it together. They accepted me. I was very happy just to be involved. Then, we get to like January, February, and they say, "Shit, looks like we're going to the National League. We haven't signed up for this." So, they dropped out.'

In the meantime, Matt Porter was trying to keep the remaining staff at the club informed and on board. He could see a glint of light at the end of the tunnel.

'We wanted to come in in the January because I think if we'd have had that transfer window, we could have made sure we didn't lose our league status,' says Porter. 'But it drifted. In the end, I was saying to people, "Look, I know it's shit. I know you're not getting paid. I know they're useless. But just trust me on this. This has got every chance."'

'It was left with me and Matt,' continues Travis. 'I remember thinking, well, we'll have to carry on because this is so bad. And then I had this very fortuitous phone call.'

The call came from Steve Powell – the commercial manager of Houston Dynamo FC. He was enquiring if Dunkin' might be interested in sponsoring the franchise. Travis declined. Instead, he asked Powell one of the most important questions he'd ever asked anyone in his life. Did he know anyone who might want to put money into Leyton Orient?

'He gave me three names,' says Travis. 'And one of them was Kent.'

It's time for 'y'all' to meet Kent Teague.

Adding an extra drawl or two

The exact date is sketchy, but it was sometime in April 2017. The night Kent Teague first saw Brisbane Road. He'd been dreaming about it since childhood. Sort of.

I first speak to Teague over Zoom, 9am Texas time. I put it to him that he has the most American-sounding name you could possibly have. Thankfully, he laughs.

'Correct. Absolutely. And the thing is, it's not just American. It's *super* Texan. I am TEXAS, TEXAS, TEXAS, TEXAS, TEXAS. I'm more Texas than Leyton Orient has history.'

He's right. He is Texas. Imagine the most Texan-sounding voice you can and add an extra drawl or two. That's Kent Teague. His family literally come from a town called Teague in Texas, showing up in 1845. They've remained in Texas ever since. It's absurd he would ever visit Brisbane Road.

'Completely, it makes no sense. It makes *no* sense. And yet, when I'm at Leyton Orient it makes perfect sense. I love it. It's crazy.'

The son of a dentist and a 'stay-at-home mom', he grew up in a suburb of Dallas with dreams of becoming a professional golfer. Among other things.

'I always knew I wanted to be wealthy. That was number one. But I'd started writing down things I wanted and reading them every day, when I was about 14 or 15. So I talked myself into a whole bunch of stuff. And one of the things I talked myself into was being a part of a pro franchise. That's how I eventually get to Leyton Orient, because I'd written it down 35 years ago. I wanted to own a pro sports team.'

After university in San Antonio ('My degree is a business major and a computer science minor. And that is exactly who I am. I am a business major with a technology minor'), Teague achieved his dream of becoming a professional golfer. For a year he played on the PGA Tour, but found he didn't have the temperament, or the desire, to remain. 'I was good enough to be there, but I wasn't good enough to stay there,' he says. 'I don't have the right mental structure to play professional golf. I'm too aggressive. I'm too impatient. I'm too emotional.'

CHAPTER 8

His time on the tour also exposed just how important his number one priority was: becoming wealthy. In golf, if you don't win, you don't get paid. And although he was good, he wasn't quite good enough.

'I either wanted to be one of the greats, like Tiger [Woods], or I wasn't going to do it. I'm persistent in some ways. And then I'm a quitter in others. I want to perform and compete at an elite level. I want that for Leyton Orient. I want that in my children, you know? But there are some places where you're like, man, you got to ease up.'

He doesn't ease up very often. After quitting golf, Teague found his calling, moving into software development. He worked for Microsoft throughout the 90s, before working on a 'co-hosting facility' – 'where the cloud lives today'. A further series of successful tech and software businesses later ('I've had four different companies that are on the Inc. 500 ... the 500 fastest-growing companies in America'), Teague found himself the owner of a legal technology business with a subsidiary in London. He sold it in 2015, but it was through this company he first heard of Leyton Orient.

'The guy that was running the company for us in the UK was Simon Manton. I asked him when we sold the business: "Hey, I know you love English football – you got any clubs I should look at?" He sent me a list of 13.'

Manton, a Walsall fan, included Leyton Orient on the list. After initially looking at American sports – NBA, Major League Baseball, NASCAR, and then being offered an ice hockey team in Dallas ('My accent does not fit English football and it sure doesn't fit hockey – I'm not Canadian or Russian!'), Teague made written offers to two Major League Soccer sides. Nothing went through, but his interest was noticed by people on the inside – an investment banker and a mutual friend of Nigel Travis who worked at Houston Dynamo FC.

'They both called me on the same day and said, you need to call this guy Nigel Travis. He's looking at buying a club called Leyton Orient.'

Teague had already done his research. He was aware of Orient because of 'the list'. He'd already had conversations with Charlton and taken a look at Portsmouth. He'd looked at clubs in Argentina, Brazil, Colombia, Costa Rica and Germany. This was a man ready to go when the right club came along. Teague and Travis arranged a call.

'Nigel wanted to do something about Leyton Orient. He wasn't sure at that time that he really wanted to be the primary owner from a financial investment perspective. So, we just had a conversation about Leyton Orient and about his history. He had lived in Dallas. I knew some people that he knew, we had common friends. We kind of knew of each other. Forty-five minutes into the conversation I asked Nigel what he thought the deal would be with Becchetti. He told me what the number was. I told him I'd wire the money tomorrow.'

Teague was ready.

'This is how I am. I do a lot of work to see what the opportunity should be. And the minute it shows up, it's over. I execute on the opportunity. Immediately.'

Teague flew to Boston, meeting Travis at his Dunkin' Donuts office, before heading to his house. He stayed for two nights, and they just clicked. 'We got on really well. I think it makes his wife nervous. Makes my wife nervous too.'

They agreed to do the deal, Travis bringing Teague up to speed on the history of the club and the madness of the Becchetti regime.

'I knew what we were getting in to. The main thing that Nigel communicated to me was that Leyton Orient was worth it. I mean, that's what it comes down to. Is it worth it? And he communicated that it was worth it in a number of different ways. He had a good relationship with

Barry Hearn. So, the stadium was something we'd be able to figure out. We had a solid fanbase. It had a solid history. It was worth doing, even though we were going to start out in the National League. I didn't know any better. "So what? National League? It don't mean anything to me. Are we in a league? Yeah. Is it a professional league? Great. Let's go." I was dumb enough not to know better, and I'm still dumb enough not to know better.'

Teague plays up to the dumb American persona – 'I love making fun of it. I'm like, why the hell do y'all listen to me? I don't even know what offside means!' – but he truly cares about Leyton Orient. He knew it would be worth it. He just didn't know how much.

'Nigel undersold it,' says Teague. 'I promise you that.'

It's easy to fall in love

Back to that chilly night in April.

In secret, Kent Teague flew to London to meet Nigel Travis and Matt Porter. They had big plans to discuss: the takeover of Leyton Orient Football Club. Porter picked Teague up from his hotel in a taxi and they met up with Travis.

'I hadn't been to London in years and years and years,' says Teague. 'I didn't have any idea where he was taking me. I mean, I had *no* idea where we were going.'

Although Teague suggests they may have eaten somewhere in Whitechapel, Porter knows they arrived at an Italian restaurant of Travis's choice, somewhere in Notting Hill. Travis left soon after the meal to 'catch a flight or something', leaving Porter to entertain his new associate from Texas, who had no idea which part of the UK he was in ('He could have taken me to Gillingham for all I knew!').

'It was the first time I'd met Kent,' says Porter. 'And I had to look after him. I didn't know what to do. I'm thinking, I've got this multimillionaire from Texas sat in front of me and I said to my wife, "Look, I don't know what's going to happen tonight ... You know, I might be out a while." So, I said to him, "Do you want to go to the stadium? You've never been to the stadium. You can't buy a club if you don't know what the stadium is like."'

Teague agreed and Porter phoned club secretary Lindsey Martin.

'It was like nine o'clock at night, midweek, evening. I said to Lindsey, this sounds really weird, but I've got one of the potential buyers with me. Can you just get down the stadium? I know this is awkward, but can you come and turn the lights on?'

Thankfully, Lindsey and Ada live just around the corner from Brisbane Road. It was 'Not a problem, see you soon.'

But how to get over to Leyton with a Texan multimillionaire?'

'Notting Hill's on the Central line, right?' says Porter. 'But I thought, this guy's too rich. He's not going to want to go on the tube. So, I said, we'll get a cab.'

It was a bad choice.

'This cab took so long to get to the stadium,' continues Porter. 'And I'm trying to keep the conversation going. I can tell he's sitting there thinking, "What am I doing? I've sat in this traffic in London at ten o'clock at night going to a football stadium!" And we got to the stadium after way too long. If we had been on the tube, it would take half an hour. And now, knowing Kent like I do, he'd have preferred it on the tube.'

'Matt and I hit it off really well,' says Teague. 'He's amazing. He and I just were talking about it all. It was fascinating hearing all the stuff from his perspective on the club and how it should be run and what we should do. It was a great conversation.'

Teague had already made his mind up to invest, even without seeing the stadium. But walking into Brisbane Road sharpened the focus of what he was about to do, even if he had to use his imagination.

'You know ... it's a building, right. It's a building. So, when you go into an office or any sort of stadium or anything, and there's nobody there and none of the lights are on and all that – it's fairly lifeless. You have to imagine what it would be like to have people in it.'

Porter and Lindsey Martin turned the lights on and walked Teague around. A mega-rich Texan walking around a small football stadium hidden away in east London. 'What I mainly remember is, "Here's a clock." This is Nigel's great grandfather's clock or his grandfather's clock or his dad's clock or something.'

'It was a bit bizarre,' says Porter. But it did the job. And Teague got it. This club had history. It was real.

'I could tell that Lindsey was super dedicated to the club,' says Teague. 'And there was a "wow I can see this". Brisbane Road is an intimate setting for an emotional experience. A gem of a stadium. You can't get within 24 rows at West Ham. And you can't sit further than 24 rows to the pitch at Leyton Orient. So, if you want an intimate experience, Leyton Orient is the best spot in the world.'

If it sounds like a backhanded compliment, it isn't. Teague was sold by the magic of Brisbane Road. By the passion of Lindsey Martin and Matt Porter. By the stories told by Nigel Travis. A club in the heart of a working-class community, surrounded by terraced houses and family homes. A club with almost as much history as the Teague family itself. A club he could fall in love with.

As Teague says, 'Sometimes it's easy to fall in love with something when you're around people who really love it.'

The reign of error

With Teague in place, a potential takeover was on.

Travis would be the chairman while Teague would be vice-chairman and principal investor. Travis's colleague at Dunkin', Richard Emmet, also got involved, as did Travis's son, David. Entrepreneur and fellow Orient fan Marshall Taylor reached out and was invited to join the team. As ever, Matt Porter would play an intrinsic role.

All they had to do was get the deal done.

'We met every single morning five days a week at 5.30am, which for Kent was 4.30,' says Travis, who was still working at Dunkin' at the time. 'We did that for probably three or four months to prepare for it. And then dealing with Mr B was an absolute freaking nightmare. One day it was on, the next day it wasn't. Then he suddenly phoned me up and said, "OK, I've decided to do it." And then we had the negotiations.'

The actual details of the negotiations are still confidential. Porter stayed out of it.

'He wouldn't have wanted to have seen me and I wouldn't have wanted to have seen him. And it wasn't the sort of business transaction I was used to conducting. It wasn't my money. It was Nigel and Kent's money. But I just saw it as my responsibility to help furnish them with as many facts and as much information as possible, and also help them build a plan for how the club could be rescued. Because I know how to run this football club.'

It was around this time that Teague launched 'Cryptic Kent' on Twitter.

'I wanted to start communicating to the fanbase that everything was going to be OK. And that we were going to fix it. That we would make it better.'

Meanwhile, Travis was on the front line leading the negotiations with Becchetti and his team. It was an illuminating experience.

'We're in this big law room, and on our side we had a young lawyer called Geoff Cunningham,' explains Travis.

CHAPTER 8

'And we had a finance guy called Trevor Birch. Now Trevor is the CEO of the [English Football] League. At one stage, Mr B said, "What the hell do you know about football?" That tells you about our previous owner more than anything.'

Despite the difficulties, the deal was done. On 22 June 2017, Francesco Becchetti sold Leyton Orient to Eagle Investments, a business consortium led by Nigel Travis and principal investor Kent Teague.

'We couldn't do any due diligence because there was nothing to look at,' continues Travis. 'We bought a club with eight players, no training ground, no season tickets sold, and spectacularly, no bank account.'

For the fans, it didn't matter. As podcast host Matt Simpson says, 'Before actually thinking about who had taken over, just the fact that Becchetti had sold was cause for celebration.'

After three years, nine full-time managers and two shattering, devastating relegations, it was done.

Becchetti's reign of error was over.

The other guy has gone!

They call it 'Orient Day'.

'[The] 22nd of June 2017. 4.45pm,' says Paul Levy. 'That's when Matt Porter released the announcement on the website and on socials. I'll never forget it.'

Every year, Paul and his co-host of *The Orient Outlook Podcast* mark 'Orient Day' with a post on their social media. 'Happy Orient Day' to all those who celebrate. The anniversary of the day Nigel Travis and Kent Teague saved Leyton Orient.

'I was sat at my job working in Holborn and I just remember sitting there looking at this statement that had come from Twitter,' says Paul. 'I stopped what I was doing. And I just remember looking on my massive monitor at this statement that the club had been saved. Lifelong fan Nigel Travis and Kent Teague through his investment fund had basically saved the club and we were under new ownership. And the other guy had gone.'

The post on Twitter is a simple one, written in all caps. Posted via Matt Porter's phone at exactly 4.46pm, presumably using his personal data plan; they didn't have the wifi code for the office.

'CONSORTIUM LED BY NIGEL TRAVIS PURCHASES LEYTON ORIENT. READ MORE HERE:' screamed the Tweet, linking through to a statement on the club website.

'I remember just sitting back in my chair and that was like a "wow" moment,' continues Paul. 'It's one of those, you'll "always remember where you were when…" And I will always remember the exact spot in that office, where I was and what I was doing. I saw it flash up on my phone, and I just wanted to see it with my own eyes on a big screen – that we'd been saved and that we were safe and that we weren't out of business and that we had a club to support.'

Paul's joy was reflected in the entire fanbase. A collective exhale that the nightmare was over. Replies to the club's message reference tears of joy and relief. There's also some glee at Becchetti's parting words.

'I am leaving it in good hands with Nigel Travis,' says Becchetti. 'I invested a great deal in the club in good faith and have delivered the club to Nigel Travis and his consortium without any debts to the banks, without arrears for taxes and salaries and in a normal situation with its suppliers.'

Predictably, the previous ownership is jeered off with four letter words and multiple exclamation marks.

'Thanks for fuck all, Becchetti you wanker,' just about sums it up.

CHAPTER 8

Dunkin' 'O'nuts

It only lasts 78 seconds, but it is enough. On 25 June 2017, a video appears on the club's official YouTube channel. Simply titled, 'A message from Leyton Orient Club Chairman Nigel Travis', it's the video every Orient fan has been waiting for.

Travis sits at a table draped in various Orient shirts from the recent past. In front of him is a tub of Baskin Robbins ice cream and a Dunkin' Donuts coffee cup. In the background, on a green screen, is an image of the North Stand at Brisbane Road. The club badge is burned on to the video at the top right of the screen.

Travis looks relaxed in his suit jacket and blue shirt as he introduces himself to the fanbase.

'Hi everyone, my name is Nigel Travis. I happen to be the chairman and CEO of Dunkin' Brands, that's Baskin Robbins and Dunkin' Donuts. However, I'm here to talk about my love for Leyton Orient.'

After showing off his collection of shirts, shirts collected from his '59 years following the Os', Travis tells the world, or east London at least, the plan.

'So, we've formed a consortium, you've probably heard about it. Our goal is to buy Leyton Orient out of our love for the club. Our goal is to return it to the winning days of the past. So "Up the Os", and we'll be looking to build a sustainable culture for the future that's about fun, about community, whilst maintaining our great heritage as London's second oldest professional football club.'

He puts out an appeal for the fans to continue their 'great job' supporting the team, to buy a season ticket and to bring their friends to 'come out and see the new Leyton Orient'.

'We're gonna return to the good days of the past. It may take a year or two to get there, but we're confident we can do it, we've got a great plan. And we know with your loyalty and your support we will fulfil our dreams. Thank you.'

With that, the video fades to black.

Looking back at the video, Nigel is fully aware of its importance. 'I was so proud, so excited,' he says. 'Actually, it's giving me shivers just talking about it.'

As one comment underneath the video says, 'Already better than the last lot!'

And then nothing happened

As it was confirmed that Eagle Investments had completed the purchase of Leyton Orient, neither of the club's new custodians were in the country. Travis was in America, while Teague was on a family trip to Australia. He celebrated the news with his wife and daughters by ordering pizza to their hotel room. The following day they were flying home. It was a memorable occasion.

'I get up and I go to the airport in Australia. I'm standing in a line to get on to an airplane and there's another line of people getting on planes in Australia. And three Leyton Orient fans come from this line to my line. They say, "Oh my God, are you Kent Teague?!"'

Teague was delighted to talk to them – Cryptic Kent finally outed as one of the saviours of their club. The meeting left a real impression on the Teague family.

'When they walked away, after 15 minutes, my wife said, "Oh my God, our lives have changed."'

Back in London, Matt Porter walked through the door as a member of the Leyton Orient board once again.

'Lindsey was there, a big smile on her face. I'd written the press release to announce the sale, but we didn't have the login details for the website. We got that and agreed the time to upload it. Then nothing happened. Because there was nothing that could have happened. There was nobody there. [It was] Lindsey, Steve Dixon, who was the commercial manager and Liz, Lindsey's daughter, who was doing some

CHAPTER 8

of the admin at the time. I don't think there was anybody else there.'

'I was in communication with Matt,' says Teague. 'But there wasn't really anything I could, you know, physically do. I didn't live in the UK. I didn't live in London. I was more like the cheerleader. "Everything's going to be OK. It's all good. We have money. Everybody will get paid."'

Despite the new owners not being in the country, the club having a skeleton administration staff, a squad of eight players, no actual training ground and, unbelievably, no bank account, the new ownership were confident.

'I was excited,' says Travis. 'I mean, I had Kent who had turned around several companies; Marshall (Taylor – more on him soon) who's kind of an entrepreneur; Matt who knew the place inside out, and I had turned around Dunkin' very successfully. I think we went in with a fair amount of confidence.'

'Look, I knew what we were getting into,' adds Teague. 'I knew it was worse than it was being presented. "So, we don't have a bank account. That's a little unusual, but OK. We don't have a credit card. OK. We don't have this. We don't have that. OK, well, let's go get it!" I wasn't concerned from a business perspective. I wired three years' worth of money. Day one. Three years' worth of money. Day. One. Enough to buy the club and enough to run the club for three years. Everybody just takes a deep breath and relaxes.'

Still, Travis, who had also transferred his own money, wasn't underestimating the task ahead.

'Despite all the knowledge Matt has,' says Travis. 'Nothing can prepare you for taking over a football club. It's unique. It's like no other business. Everything happens so quick. Crazy things happen at football clubs. I think we were shocked that nothing had been done about the next season.'

As Travis notes to me, Porter had the knowledge to run the club, but he also has a high-profile day job – chief executive of the Professional Darts Corporation. There was only so much he could do, only so much time he could devote to getting Leyton Orient up and running again.

Which is why I find myself on a video call, talking to the man who, in Matt Porter's words, 'came in to sort it all out'.

Let's meet Marshall Taylor.

How to spunk away your children's inheritance

When Marshall Taylor informed his partner he was joining Nigel Travis's consortium to save Leyton Orient, she wasn't happy.

'I was in the doghouse for, I'm going to say, six weeks,' he says. 'What are you doing? That's the children's inheritance you're just spunking away!' was the message he received.

Unlike Nigel Travis, Taylor isn't a lifelong Orient fan. He'd never worked in football, like Matt Porter. He never wanted to run a football club, like Kent Teague. He's an entrepreneur and he took a punt on the Os.

Starting as a computer programmer, he had launched three software startups before the age of 24. After a period working for Deloitte, he then got involved with a fashion startup called Palace. Running the e-commerce side of the business, he was part of the team that scaled the company to a nine-figure sum from a £10,000 investment. It was a global success, and as Taylor says, 'We didn't spend a single dollar on advertising.'

It was during these financially fruitful entrepreneurial days that Taylor found himself looking for an escape from the stress of his working life. He found a different kind of stress instead: watching Leyton Orient.

'I was grinding seven days a week, all hours,' he says. 'And sometimes on a midweek I wanted to go and watch a game

CHAPTER 8

of football, just to kind of unwind. I was living in Hackney, in Victoria Park, and Orient was one of the only London teams that you could actually turn up on the turnstiles with cash and go and watch a game. Whereas if you wanted to go and watch an Arsenal or West Ham or a Tottenham game, it was all sold out. So, I started paying cash on the turnstile in the South Stand.'

Without realising it, suddenly he was a Leyton Orient supporter. It happens.

'You went two or three times for a couple of seasons,' he says. 'Then you start to go four or five times, and after eight, nine, whatever it is, you get the bug. You become the firm. You start looking on the forum. You start getting involved and buying merchandise. Cold Tuesday nights in the South Stand on my own ... It was great. I just sat there. An escapism from work and pressure.'

It was in the middle of Francesco Becchetti's final season that Taylor first took his young kids to a match. 'They were two and four. And I took them because I knew what was going on behind the scenes, and I thought to myself, "This could be the last time we could go as a family to the game."'

The plight of the club was enough for Taylor to reach out to Nigel Travis and offer his services. As he freely admits, he had no real interest in running a football club, but there was *something* about that little club that he'd been jumping on the Central line to watch for a few years. He sent Travis a message.

'It was a cold email. And then a flight out to Boston to meet his family, a few phone calls. And then I was part of the consortium. I agreed to invest some money and said, "Look, I think I've got some skills." And, quite importantly, we needed some UK boots on the ground.'

As Matt Porter says, Taylor was 'around from day one' as part of the team that met every day for six months at 5.30am,

Boston time, working on ways to get Becchetti to agree to the sale.

'It was like trying to deal with no one else I've ever dealt with before,' he explains. 'Nigel's obviously met many, many more powerful CEOs than I have. Even he was struggling. It was off the scale how difficult it was. I think when we first started, we were probably naive. We thought we could get it done pretty quickly. At the time, he was under real fan pressure. The debts were mounting. The bad press was mounting. But with him [Becchetti], he was just delusional. He didn't care.'

The pressure on Taylor and the team began to build.

'Those calls were quite frustrating in the end. We probably did hundreds and hundreds of hours of calls over a six-month period. The calls were a minimum an hour, sometimes two or three. And it was just a rollercoaster. I think in the end, we'd made five or six offers. Nigel had flown over from the States five times to sign the deal, only to be told on the day, or even in the hour before, "the deal's off".'

Over the intervening months, it was agreed that Taylor would take on interim CEO duties. He freely admits it wasn't a dream role.

'A few of my personal friends after we took over the club, were like, "Oh, it must be amazing being a football club CEO." And I was like, "It's the worst thing ever."'

It's not surprising. The club he was walking in to work at was barely functioning. From his very first day, Leyton Orient was, in his own words, 'a complete burning ship'.

Marshall Taylor had to put the fire out.

Replacing the light bulbs

The first day was a shock.

Taylor received a call from Nigel Travis informing him that the deal was done. They were going in the following day, 9am.

CHAPTER 8

'We didn't know whether there would be electricity on. We didn't know how many staff would still be there. He [Becchetti] allowed us to do no due diligence. But I can remember walking in, getting out of the Uber and looking through reception. I could see the lights on. I thought, "Well, that's a good start, there's electrics."'

The electricity may have been on, but the lights were barely working.

'I can remember walking into reception and loads of the light bulbs were gone. It was dark and dingy. I got Lindsey to get all the staff that were still in the stadium together in the office. They were probably thinking, "Who the hell are you?!"'

Matt Porter was there as well. He introduced the club's new interim CEO to the remaining staff. Taylor did his best to give a rousing speech.

Formalities done, it was time to get on with the job.

'My remit was to try and give the new CEO who was coming in a blank sheet of paper on their day one. Then they could actually deal with the football club – starting to raise revenue and move it forward.'

That blank sheet of paper seemed a long way off on that first day. It was like sweeping a crime scene. On day two, they had to call in forensics.

'We had to make sure that we were covered,' says Taylor. '[That] there wasn't any money laundering that could be connected with us. We had to spend a quarter of a million pounds, maybe even more than that, on four or five forensic accountants. They sat there for six weeks and pored over every single invoice. Every single thing to make sure that we weren't exposing ourselves to anything.'

While the accountants got to work, Taylor found himself hitting the phones. He called every county court in the UK with the same introduction and the same questions, 'Hi, we're

Leyton Orient Football Club limited. Do we owe anyone money? Is anyone taking us to court? Is there any CCJs [County Court Judgements], any winding up petitions?'

As Taylor explains, the process was painstaking, but crucial. 'We didn't even know who we owed money to. They [Becchetti's team] gave us an Excel spreadsheet that was just, "We owe this person this money." It was totally inaccurate and a load of it made up. I think mainly because they'd lost complete control. They didn't know themselves.'

While juggling the nation's county courts, Taylor was also trying to make sure Leyton Orient's long-suffering staff actually got paid. There was money from Teague and the investors, but no club bank account.

'We had nothing,' he explains. 'When it came to payday, a couple of days later, I was spending everything on my personal card. Anything the club needed, my personal card, and Nigel's. I was logged into his Coutts personal bank account, and we were paying people, setting them up on his bank account, and paying them individually.'

Taylor and Teague found themselves back-paying staff to March.

'You can imagine all the people that were owed money, the staff, all of the stewards, all of the matchday hospitality. When you set up a new payee on your bank it takes a couple of minutes to put all the details in. You have to go through security again. Can you imagine doing that about 280 times? It took two or three days just to sit there and punch in everyone's details. And obviously, after you're working all hours, if you add an extra zero on to someone's payment … it can be absolute chaos.'

There were also the functional things, the things none of the new leadership had even thought about before taking control of the club: food for the players when they started training, filling the kitchen with new utensils, replacing

CHAPTER 8

training equipment. 'Then obviously, lots of people had left,' continues Taylor. 'There were loads of roles we needed to fill. And this is not the football side, just the general business side.'

Alongside all of this, there was the small matter of an unpaid mobile phone bill.

'I call Vodafone up and I'm like, "How much do we owe you?" "Oh, you owe us £37,000." And I'm like, "What? For the year?" And they're like, "No, that was for last month." I was working every hour God sent. We all were just trying to get the football club functioning again.'

While Marshall Taylor and the team were trying to get the club through the first few weeks, Kent Teague and Nigel Travis were also thinking about the longer-term future.

They had devised a plan. It was one of the most important decisions they made.

What's the Italian for 'y'all'?

Everyone knows it as the six-year plan, but Kent Teague would like to put the record straight.

'Woah, woah, woah, woah, woah. Eight-year plan. Six to eight years. Three to four years in the National League, three to four years in League Two, then we'll be in League One.'

Either way, it's gone down in history as the famous six-year plan: the mission statement pulled together by Travis and Teague at the start of their tenure. A tangible plan to give a hungry fanbase realistic hope for the future after years of mismanagement and decline.

'I'd studied enough to know that the worst thing to do as a new American owner was to come in and say, "Two years and we'll have you back in League One." Our fans would have been like, "You guys are the biggest bunch of idiots we've ever met." So, in order to garner trust and excitement, it's better to set forth a plan that seems to be mostly realistic and not to overpromise.'

Teague describes himself as naturally 'not an overpromiser', but for a man with such obvious ambition and drive, you could go as far to say that he sometimes chooses to lean into pessimism rather than optimism.

'I'm the one that says, "Man, I don't know if we're ever going to get out of the National League." And then everybody's like, "What?!" I'm like, "All right. Well, maybe three or four years, all right?"'

For Travis, he was thinking even longer-term from the very start. 'I've only got one goal – that Leyton Orient is thriving, whatever that means, in 100 years' time. We said that when we bought the club. We've only got 94 years to go.'

Despite this worthy ambition, Teague is also very conscious that Becchetti had promised the world and delivered nothing but relegation and near bankruptcy.

'Becchetti basically said, "Y'all, we were just one kick away. I'm going to put you in the Premier League in three years." Well, he put us somewhere in three years! But it wasn't the Premier League. It was the other way. We were reacting and responding to what Becchetti had done.'

Whether the Italian said 'Y'all' or not, Teague has a point. Orient had a plan and the new owners let the fans know. The club had been saved. There was a tangible ambition.

The only problem: there weren't any players.

Just a spreadsheet

The new owners needed some help. Someone who knew football. With Matt Porter and Marshall Taylor on the ground, Nigel Travis and Kent Teague could rebuild the club. But they needed someone to rebuild the team.

One man fitted the bill: former Orient player, coach and manager Martin Ling.

I meet Ling at the club's Chigwell training ground. It's shared with the Old Chigwellians, the clubhouse for the

CHAPTER 8

various sports teams associated with alumni of Chigwell School, Essex. It doesn't feel like a professional football club's training ground. Wooden plaques adorn the cricket pavilion walls, listing past captains and honours, all for the Old Chigwellians. Through the large floor-to-ceiling windows, I watch the first team train while drinking a coffee. Ling finishes his prior appointment. When he's done, he greets me warmly.

'You can ask any question about anything,' he says. 'It's not a problem.'

We have a lot to talk about.

When I first started going to Brisbane Road as a teenager in the late 90s, Martin Ling had recently signed from Swindon Town, a team he helped get promoted to the Premier League. As an attacking midfielder playing under future England manager and genuine footballing genius Glenn Hoddle, Ling had been part of the Swindon team that defeated Leicester City in the First Division play-off final, earning promotion to the Premier League for the 1993/94 season.

I remember Ling as one of Orient's best players. I saw him play at Wembley in 1999 as Orient lost 1-0 to Scunthorpe in the old Third Division play-off final. I then saw him as manager, leading the team at Oxford in 2006 when his hard-working Orient secured a dramatic final-day promotion to League One. He was a man who knew the club. But did he know how to save it?

Matt Porter had phoned Ling in the March before the takeover. Travis and Teague needed someone to pull together a 'football philosophy' and, as Ling tells me, provide an indication of 'the costs that would incur.'

'That led me to me doing a famous Martin Ling spreadsheet of players, for what it should cost in the National League,' he says. 'I was just doing Matt a favour. We'd been close when we were here, and we kept in touch. And then out of the blue, he went, "Can you come to Nigel's flat in Notting Hill to present what you've done?"'

Ling met with Travis, Porter, Teague and Taylor at Travis's apartment in Notting Hill. 'A Tardis' of an apartment according to Ling. Over coffee, he talked through the potential plans.

'I talked about football in general,' says Ling. 'I was instructed to keep Kent engaged, because they wanted him to come on board. He was like a mad Texan with a million questions coming at me. Some of his questions were to do with not knowing "soccer". I answered all the questions. And as I was driving home back to my house, out of Notting Hill, the phone rang, and Matt said, "They really like you." I said, "Oh, that's nice." He said, "They would like you to be part of it." And I was like, "Don't tell me they want me to be the manager."'

They didn't. They had another offer for him: director of football. This was something Ling was prepared to consider. After discussing the proposal with his wife, he decided to accept. But he needed to discuss things with another woman first: club secretary Lindsey Martin.

'Obviously she was my secretary before. I spoke to her because she was on the verge of leaving. She'd been offered a job elsewhere. Matt had been in constant contact with Lindsey, so she was feeding back how bad it was. And I said, "Look, it's going to happen. I'm coming back in. This is what I'm going to do. But I need you."'

Lindsey agreed to stay, and Leyton Orient had a new director of football.

But there was a reason Matt Porter hadn't offered Ling the manager's role in the first place. Three years earlier he had walked out on his dream job as manager of Swindon and then walked straight into rehab.

CHAPTER 8

I won't be a football manager ever again

Martin Ling was manager of Swindon Town for just 56 days.

After leaving Orient in 2009, Ling went on to manage Cambridge United and Torquay United before his brief stint back at Swindon, a club he held much affection for. He was battling depression in every job.

Ling was first admitted to The Priory while managing at Torquay in 2013, later telling the BBC that due to the levels of medication he was on during his first few weeks, his time there was 'a blur'. Two years later, he was back in rehab. He'd had no choice but to leave his job, despite leading Swindon to a great start in League One.

'That was the hardest decision ever,' he tells me. 'It was tough because I played there for five years. It was something I dreamed of doing, but I knew my mental health wouldn't hold up. I would have got it [depression] whatever I was doing. But I did say to Caroline, my wife, I won't be a football manager ever again.

'I gave up alcohol while I was in The Priory. On the vice of using it as a coping mechanism. And then the second time I got it [depression], I was four years sober. That really threw me.'

As we talk, the first-team squad are piling into the pavilion, diving into the lunchtime burritos that have been laid on by the club chef. Ling talks about his illness willingly and comfortably. The lads bustle and chat around us.

'I go out and quite regularly do talks for depression in sport,' continues Ling. 'There are quite a few people that get depression when they can't do the sport they used to do any more. If you've played professional football from 16 to 34 and you've had all them highs, how do you search out that high again? Every day I battle with it. But it's a battle I win every day. That's how I look at it now.'

For Matt Porter and Orient's new leadership team, Ling's struggles were never a barrier to offering him a job.

'Matt was brilliant around my illness,' Ling says. 'People were scared to pick the phone up. But Matt always picked the phone up. So, we kept a friendship.'

Having worked with him during his time as CEO under Barry Hearn, Porter knew that Ling could handle the director of football role. 'He quickly became part of the plan,' Porter says. And once Ling thought about it, being a director of football was the perfect position for him.

'When I looked at the job, I had the skillset they required. A good spreadsheet just looks like a good 4-4-2. That was ingrained in me through Barry [Hearn]. When I first took the manager's job in 2003, he said that within a year he was pulling away, and he wanted me to take over completely with all the negotiations. I'd call him in if an agent got sticky – then I'd put Barry into bat. But he taught me how to work a budget, how to do it on a spreadsheet, how to negotiate.'

When Ling first signed for Hearn as a player in 1996, he threatened to walk away twice, negotiating hard for the best contract. He recalls Hearn describing it as one of the hardest negotiations he had with a player. 'I never had an agent. So, from the age of 20, I was negotiating for myself,' Ling adds.

Despite the role being perfect, Ling still had a decision to make. He'd managed to build a life away from professional football, running a coaching company. 'I just started to get myself back on my feet,' he says. 'But the urge to be back in the game was too strong.'

The board's first appointment, Ling was a vital part of the team that saved the club. But, I ask, did the club also save him?

'Yeah, I'll go with that,' he says. 'I think it's helped rebuild me. I thought I was finished with professional football. I had two big bouts of depression, and it stains your CV. But one

CHAPTER 8

of the greatest things was when I agreed to take the job, I told them [Travis and Teague] about my mental health. They said they knew. I told them about my coping strategies, which were alcohol, that are no longer alcohol. "Don't care. We worry about the person and what they do." The attitude to my illness by the people that are in charge made my illness normal. The saving of Leyton Orient and the saving of me go hand in hand.'

Martin Ling got to work.

'I ain't got a physio!'

Those first few weeks were a flurry of activity, a blur of necessary action. With Marshall Taylor as interim CEO, working to make Leyton Orient a functioning football business, Martin Ling hit the phones, working to give the club a functioning football team. The first task: to secure the training ground. Like most things, it had been neglected by the previous regime. Old Chigwellians had not been paid.

'They were on the verge of going to another club,' explains Ling. 'So, I spoke to them directly and they believed what I was saying, "We'll pay all the bills."'

Training ground secured, Ling's next task was to find someone who could lead the team in training while a new manager was found. He knew exactly the man for the job. A man who had risen through the ranks as a player in the academy and then as a coach when Ling was Orient manager: his former first-team coach at Swindon, Ross Embleton.

I speak to Ross over video call. An Orient fan since he was six or seven years old ('Orient was in the family. It's just always been part of my life'), he remembers the moment Ling called, just as he was walking into an interview for another job. But as soon as Embleton spoke to his former gaffer, his mind was made up.

'It was a no-brainer,' he tells me. 'There was nowhere else I was going over Orient.'

He remembers walking into the stadium on his first day back at his boyhood club.

'Martin sat down, and he said to me, "Mate, you've got a job here, but I can't tell you what it's going to be. All I know is it's going to be related to football. It might be under-18s coach. It might be back in the academy. It might be assistant manager. But there's a job, I just can't tell you what it is, and I can't give you a contract to tell you what your job's going to be." And I was like, "No, that's good enough for me. I'm here and we're ready to go."'

Coach in place, Ling needed to find some footballers. He didn't even have enough to field an 11-a-side team. 'I looked at what players we had, which was about nine,' he says. 'And no one over the age of 19 at the time. We're coming in, 22 June and we've got no pre-season games. We've got nothing.'

Orient needed to get a squad assembled quickly. Ling employed Steve Foster as his new chief scout, sourcing available players from the upper and lower age brackets of the available professionals. 'All the players that were 23 to 29, they're gone,' explains Ling. 'All the good products – gone.' The most desirable players, already snapped up in the transfer window. Ling needed to find some hidden gems.

However, new problems kept arising.

'When we got to the training ground, three days before we started pre-season training, it was like a lightbulb moment. "I ain't got a physio." It was a case of building the staff around Ross and then building a team of players. It was probably the most hectic period of anything I've ever done in football.'

'When we walked in the first day, we obviously had no squad, but we didn't even have a bag of balls!' says Embleton. 'I remember Ada saying to me, "I know they're somewhere,

CHAPTER 8

but when we get to the lockup container at Chigwell, I'm not quite sure what's going to be there and what's not."'

With young prospects like Dan Happe and Josh Koroma already committed to the club, Ling and his team added as much experience as possible. Striker David Mooney, a fan favourite of the 2014 play-off team, was quickly snapped up, as were Alex Lawless from Yeovil and fellow seasoned professional Charlie Lee from Stevenage. Lawless was soon joined from Stevenage by another former Orient player, Jobi McAnuff. Meanwhile, Embleton was joined by returning coach Danny Webb.

'I was just trying to give the squad some assurances pretty quickly,' says Embleton. 'Every day, you're going to see two or three new players. It was like, "Look, this is how it's going to work over the next little while. We're going to get you up to speed, up to fitness as quickly as possible. Who's going to be the manager? We don't know. How quickly is he going to be the manager? We don't really know. We've all just got to make the best of the scenario and get it as professional and up to scratch as quickly as possible."'

For Embleton, it felt personal.

'They were a good group of boys. They obviously cared about the club. And what we built from what we had when we walked in the door was incredible. To be able to rebuild a football club – my football club – I was so lucky.'

Doing the physical training and pre-season bleep tests for a professional football squad wasn't easy though, especially when there were no fitness coaches or sports scientists on the staff.

'We were like, "Right, has anybody got a speaker?" says Embleton. 'One morning, we used the cricket field. There was the rope to mark the boundary. "Let's send the boys on a run round the cricket pitch and we'll just time them." It couldn't get any worse, could it? It couldn't get any lower.'

Even if they were running around a cricket pitch, Jobi McAnuff remembers things moving in the right direction. 'By the time I went, we were very much on the way to assembling the squad that we wanted to put together,' he says. 'But it was a work in progress, for sure.'

'When you started to look at the players and the togetherness, you started to see something being built,' adds Ling. 'But the first year was a free year in terms of it didn't matter where we would have come. As long as we wasn't in the bottom four, that was deemed to be successful.'

The squad was soon joined by Craig Clay from Motherwell and young striker Macauley Bonne from Colchester. For the fans, it was clear that things were rapidly developing.

Matt Simpson had been reassured from the outset, 'It all just felt like we were going to get our club back. I felt like we were going to be OK. I didn't think, "Great, that means we're going to be promoted out of the National League in our first season." Just that it was going to return to the sort of things that I value in supporting Orient. That it would be run responsibly and sustainably, and by people with the right values.'

A pre-season game away at Burnham Ramblers added to the feel-good factor around the club. Billy Herring was there to see Orient win 10-0, with striker Tristan Abrahams scoring five goals. Abrahams would soon be snapped up by Championship side Norwich City, but a young second-year scholar called Ruel Sotiriou also made his mark that day. He scored two goals as a second-half substitute.

A sense of community was once again emerging.

'I remember me and my old man went over there [to Burnham],' says Billy. 'And from being so divided the following season to everyone just hugging each other. It was such a contrast.'

CHAPTER 8

It may have been 10-0, but Burnham were not a real test. A club in the Essex Senior League, the ninth tier of English football, they played at the very bottom of the pyramid.

Far sterner tests were to come.

9

Leyton Orient start their first season in non-league football with a new manager and a new squad. Former Crewe, Burnley and Barnsley defender Steve Davis is appointed as head coach on a two-year contract, a month before the start of the 2017/18 season. He has already won promotion in a play-off final as manager of Crewe Alexandra, as well as leading his team to victory in the EFL Trophy at Wembley.

Orient fans are generally optimistic.

'The first sensible appointment since [Russell] Slade. Ticks all the boxes when you look at promotions and cup final wins,' says one social media user. 'Sensible choice who comes in with fresh ideas and loads of experience. Really pleased with that,' says another.

The Coral betting social media account features a picture of former snooker world champion and Barry Hearn's most famous client, Steve Davis.

'Leyton Orient have appointed Steve Davis as their new manager. Interesting switch from snooker!' they joke.

CHAPTER 9

Bacon baps and cups of tea
Tuesday, 8 August 2017, Brisbane Road

Leyton Orient 3 Solihull Moors 1

Just getting to the first home game was an achievement.

After an opening-day defeat away at Sutton United, Orient were due to host Solihull Moors just a few days later at Brisbane Road. The new owners had only been in control of the club for six weeks.

'We only had four or five weeks to get the stadium ready,' explains Marshall Taylor. 'Money hadn't been spent on the stadium over the last year or two. We were informed there's a thing called the SAG, which is a "safety advisory group".'

The combination of police, ambulance and council representatives on the SAG board were very quick to inform the club that it would not be getting the licence it needed. The stadium needed some serious attention. It was dirty and neglected, safety markings needed to be repainted. It was a ground unfit to host even a National League match. 'There were too many problems with it, and we wouldn't be able to start the season,' says Taylor. 'We couldn't get the tradespeople in on time to do those things in order to satisfy the safety officer. So, I put a call out for all fans over a weekend period to come and help.'

The response was more than Taylor could have imagined.

'I couldn't believe it. Sixty, 70 fans arrived on that Saturday morning, and also on the Sunday. And all we gave them was bacon baps and a cup of tea! They worked all day and the next day. That was why it was such an achievement. Not just to get the playing team on there, but to get the stadium in a position where it was safe and could actually be open for our first game. And that was a joint effort. If it wasn't for them, then we wouldn't have got that first game on.'

It was worth it. Orient won their first home game of the season. Goals from captain Charlie Lee, George Elokobi and returning hero David Mooney meant that Taylor's fans walked away happy after a 3-1 victory.

Never underestimate the power of bacon baps and a cup of tea.

'We lost 6-1 at Bromley'

Nigel Travis and Kent Teague's first managerial appointment should have been a success. Steve Davis was a well-respected coach; a man who knew how to develop players.

Unfortunately for everyone involved, it just didn't work out.

Teague remembers, 'I think we all felt the first year was going to be a bit tough, because we had just thrown everything together. And I think shit hit the fan when we lost 6-1 at Bromley. "Oh, holy shit."'

Despite an encouraging start, Davis's Orient found themselves on a run which saw them win only one game in 12, teetering on the brink of the relegation zone. By mid-November, they were just three points from safety. After the chaos and frequent managerial changes of the Francesco Becchetti years, the last thing the new owners wanted to do was sack their manager with just over three months of the season completed. But they had no choice.

'Football is a results-based business,' said Travis in a statement at the time. 'And while we knew this was going to be a challenging season, we did not expect to be so close to the bottom four at this stage. We showed a lot of promise early on but that hasn't been sustained, so we felt it time to make a change.'

Kent Teague explains the brutal reality of the situation they found themselves in, 'Steve did very well. It's just he got lost because Steve was trying too hard to develop players and

CHAPTER 9

not enough to win. We didn't want to develop players. We needed out of the National League!'

Andy Gilson was starting his 30th season as Orient's regular matchday commentator. He'd been covering Orient since 1988 ('I do believe I was the longest-serving video commentator at a football club') – seeing them promoted to the old Third Division in his first full season in the job. He'd seen a lot of managers come and go.

'I felt sorry for Steve, because he was a very nice guy,' says Gilson. 'And nobody wanted him to fail, but for whatever reason, he didn't have an answer. I think he just ran out of ideas and didn't know what to do. And the club was in free fall. Something had to be done.'

Reflecting on the situation, Martin Ling can see where things went wrong. All it took were a couple of injuries for the depth of the hastily assembled squad to be exposed.

'The 11 or the 14 is quite good,' he remembers thinking at the time. 'But what have we got behind that? Obviously, it wasn't strong enough. And I feel sorry for some of the kids, because they were pushed above their station. The cracks started to show.'

Coaches Ross Embleton and Dean Brill were put in temporary charge while a new manager was found. Ling knew he had to get the next appointment right.

'The employment of managers has never changed in terms of how we do it,' Ling tells me. 'It's always a case of a coffee meeting, an hour or two, with about six, sometimes eight candidates. And then we recommend whoever we think should go to the next stage.'

There was one candidate who stood out for Ling straight away. A man who has had more impact on Leyton Orient's recent history than any other: Justin Edinburgh.

10

'There's no point in interviewing anybody else. He is the man.'

Matt Porter, after meeting Justin Edinburgh, 2017

Justin

Sometimes you just know. With Justin Edinburgh, everyone just knew.

'I had the right feel straight away,' says Martin Ling. 'We played together at Southend [in the late 1980s]. So, I knew him, but not as tight as people thought. I always say I got him his move to Tottenham,' he jokes. 'I played in front of him. I made him look good!'

As a player, Edinburgh won both the FA Cup and the League Cup while playing in the Premier League after getting his big move from Southend to Spurs in 1990. As a manager, he won promotion to the Football League with Newport County, alongside stints at Gillingham and Northampton in League One. Ling had no hesitation in putting him forward for a meeting at the Holiday Inn in Brentwood with Matt Porter and incoming CEO Danny Macklin.

'I must admit, I didn't necessarily think he was amazing beforehand,' says Porter. 'I didn't know him. Maybe he'd been manager against us and beaten us or said something. He wasn't someone who you thought, "Oh, I love him." But as soon as we did that interview, I said to Martin, "There's no doubt he'll succeed as our manager." We all agreed, and we

CHAPTER 10

referred it up to Nigel and Kent. Ling remembers immediately being impressed by Edinburgh's management style.

'I just liked his man-management from the start. I liked what he was talking about. He hadn't swallowed a coaching manual. And I'm not saying that's wrong or right, but Justin was more about the team, players, camaraderie, team ethic, the man-management side of it.'

There was only one potential sticking point.

'He wanted to employ an assistant coach to work with him,' says Ling. 'But that wasn't an option, because Ross Embleton had come in to get us out of the shit. I explained to him [Edinburgh] that we've already got our assistant coach. And if you're not happy working with our assistant coach, then there's not a job.'

Thankfully, Edinburgh was happy with the situation, and a deal could be done. What Ling didn't discuss was the history between his new manager and his assistant coach.

'When I was at Swindon, we'd played Gillingham one Boxing Day,' explains Embleton. 'The ball rolled into the tunnel. I went to grab the ball to get it back quickly and Jimmy Walker, the goalie coach, grabbed it at the same time. We sort of tussled and threw the ball back. Then Justin came flying into the tunnel, telling me he was going to smash my face in. The next morning, I got a phone call from a really good mate of mine, and he was like, "What did you do to Justin Edinburgh? He's come to my party last night, saying to me *that lairy little so-and-so, he's this, he's that.*" So, I was thinking there is no way me and Justin are hitting it off.'

Thankfully, Edinburgh and Embleton cleared the air. They got on well straight away.

'The first thing he did was shut the door, just me and him, and said, "It's me and you, now. I'm excited to work with you,"' recalls Embleton. 'Then we talked about the squad and all that sort of thing, and it started to snowball from there.'

With everyone in agreement, the deal was done.

'He was such an easy choice,' adds Porter. 'The geography [Edinburgh coming from Orient's Essex heartland], the character, the understanding of the National League, and the understanding of the league we hoped to get into. He just ticked every box.'

On 29 November 2017, Justin Edinburgh was appointed as head coach of Leyton Orient.

The next 18 months were extraordinary.

'You're a stone overweight'
On the day of his appointment, the club released an interview from their new manager. From the outset, everyone knew what they were getting.

'Everything is moving along nicely off the pitch,' said Edinburgh, to the audience on YouTube. 'Obviously what we've got to do now is try and change the results on the pitch … At the moment, the players … their decision making is clouded, and I've got to simplify that. I've got to clear that … We might not get the success straight away, but eventually we will. As long as we stick together.'

It was what everyone associated with the club needed to hear.

'I pay quite a lot of attention to how managers conduct themselves,' says Matt Simpson. 'With the press, how they describe things, the way they talk about matches, the way they talk about the team … And I was just really impressed with him to begin with. I just liked the way he talked about the club, the way he talked about what he wanted to achieve. I bought into him really quickly.'

'We've got to all pull in the right direction,' continued Edinburgh. 'That's got to come from us, staff and players,

CHAPTER 10

that when the games come, we give these fans something to believe in, and something to be proud of, and something to support ... We're all in this together now.'

For Andy Gilson, Orient's new manager seemed like a man with the right experience and personality to turn the club's fortunes around.

'Justin came in and he had a reasonable record with lower-division football clubs. And we all knew who Justin Edinburgh was. He came across as someone who wouldn't take any crap. He let everybody know that he was the boss. It's his way or the highway. He came in as quite a hard man. But we needed someone to kick the side up the backside, because we were only heading one way. We were all hopeful that this would put the brakes on the situation.'

Ada Martin clocked Edinburgh's impact immediately.

'I remember seeing him in the manager's office on the first floor. I went and introduced myself. "Just carry on what you're doing," [Edinburgh said]. You could just see he was someone who's a little more savvy. He's a Londoner, for one. He knows what to expect from the fans. He had an idea what he was going to do with the team straight away.'

One of Edinburgh's first decisions was to find an experienced goalkeeper to slot into the team ahead of Charlie Grainger and Sam Sergeant, two goalies barely out of their teens. Former Luton and Oldham man Dean Brill was on the coaching staff, but Edinburgh could see the value of his experience on the pitch. He wanted to bring him out of retirement.

'He convinced Brillo [Dean Brill], and that worked out to be a massive decision,' says Ling. 'Because he was so much the organiser. He was a really good goalkeeping coach. He was a coach behind the defence. He couldn't dive to his left. He didn't train a lot. But on the pitch, he was the biggest voice.'

Edinburgh quickly lifted the pressure off his squad.

'He just saw the weaknesses and just made little subtle changes here and there,' adds Ada. 'Everyone had a confidence he instilled in them, and it just showed.'

'It's funny, when he first came in,' continues Ling. 'Justin went, "I really like Josh Koroma, but he's stone overweight." And the first thing Justin did was to say, "You're a stone overweight. If you're going to play in my side, get your weight down, and you'll be playing." And Josh worked on that.'

Edinburgh's man-management clearly had an instant impact on the whole squad, including one of the only players who was still there and had played during the dark days of the Becchetti regime.

A young defender who was trying to make a name for himself at Leyton Orient: Dan Happe.

'Whoa, here we go'

Dan Happe first trained with Leyton Orient at 14 years old.

Signing on a scholarship two years later, he was part of the club when Russell Slade was first-team manager. He completed his scholarship while Becchetti was in charge.

Happe joins me after training for a chat over a video call. One of the club's longest-serving players with over 200 appearances, it's easy to forget he's barely in his mid-20s. It's no surprise, like all the people who have been part of the club for a while, that he's polite, intelligent and generous with his time. They bring them up well at Orient.

'I wasn't fully aware of the ins and outs of what was going on,' he says, reflecting on the Becchetti years. 'I was still fairly young at the time, so I was turning up to training and we would turn up at half nine, and there'd be no manager. Everyone looking about going, "What's going on?" And then there will be like a last-minute meeting pencilled in for half 11. We don't even train the whole morning. And everyone's in the meeting room and everyone's ranting saying, "Oh, are we going to get paid? Are we not going to get paid?" It was like that for a long time. A massive question mark every day.'

Happe made his debut against Cambridge on 8 April 2017, a 3-0 defeat on the way to relegation and the National League. Part of a young team where only three players were over the age of 20, he was then on the bench for three of the final games of that last League Two season. He was in the stands as part of the wider squad for the fan protest and pitch invasion against Colchester.

Like the Orient fans, Happe had been through it all.

'Justin was exactly what I needed,' says Happe. 'He was class. On and off the pitch. Everyone loved him. Words can't describe how good he was as a man-manager. He brought so much life to the dressing room and when we're eating at lunch and stuff. Little things that people don't see. He brought so much life there.'

Edinburgh made an impression on Happe and his teammates from his very first training session.

'It was a wet day, and we were all just going through the motions, doing a passing drill,' remembers Happe. 'Then he just switches. "F-ing this, f-ing that." And I'm going, "Whoa, here we go." That's something that was good. He could just flip a switch and then everyone's on it. He had those personal skills. Everyone respected him without a doubt.'

After defeat in his first game in charge, Justin Edinburgh and the squad immediately began to turn things around. Three wins in a row dragged the team away from any immediate danger and Orient finished the calendar year nine points clear of relegation. Finally, the club were moving in the right direction.

It was just as well. Dave Victor, covering Orient's progress for BBC London, knew the BBC was under pressure to focus their attention on other London clubs. 'BBC London had never covered a non-league team,' he says. 'But they covered this one.'

Orient needed to prove they were worth the national broadcaster's attention. The loss of coverage on the BBC would be another marker of just how far London's second-oldest professional football club had fallen, especially when other capital clubs deserved BBC London's focus.

'Barnet and Sutton were very, very unhappy,' says Victor. 'I know there was a lot of pressure. We moved to fifth from bottom, really struggling. But Sutton were pushing and Dagenham were pushing. And Barnet were really pushing. And the sports desk were getting so many complaints.'

They needn't have worried. Orient started picking up points and turning in performances. The final game of the season saw a 3-1 victory away at Gateshead, leaving the team on 60 points for the season, safely in mid-table. A platform had been laid.

All three of Orient's scorers that day were to play a key role in the club's fortunes over the following months. Macauley Bonne, signed from Colchester the previous summer, 19-year-old academy graduate Josh Koroma who had lost that stone and received a new two-year deal in return, and a man finishing his first season back at the club after rejoining the previous summer. The man Edinburgh made his captain: Jobi McAnuff.

Getting ready to fly

In 2017, Jobi McAnuff was a man with a point to prove.

'It was about going in and creating a new story for the club,' he tells me.

When Justin Edinburgh was appointed head coach in November 2017, McAnuff had just turned 36, nearly four months into his second stint at the club. The ex-Premier League star, looking for one last challenge before

CHAPTER 10

he retired, he had something to prove to himself, and to Leyton Orient.

'The club didn't see the best of me in my first spell,' he says. 'And I didn't see the best of the football club. But I went and met Kent and Nigel, and that was it for me.'

Despite the poor start to the season, McAnuff was optimistic. He could see there was a plan this time around.

'There were so many things that aligned for me, whether it was setting the record straight and showing people what I was really about, from a football point of view, but also my character. The club had a clear objective and ambition to get back in the league. It genuinely felt like a brand-new football club that was just full of positivity. It was just so nice to be a part of.'

Like the rest of the squad, McAnuff was immediately impressed by his new manager.

'Justin was someone who commanded respect. He held a room. We needed a real strong manager who understood the level. Understood that we were very much a big fish. Everybody comes to Orient and it is their cup final. And he didn't shy away from that. We had to act like we were the big fish. "We are the best team here, but you have to earn that." And that comes from the work on the training ground. That comes from making sure everything we're doing is better than everybody else. He was just someone who wasn't going to take any shit from anybody.'

Towards the end of Edinburgh's first season, he made McAnuff his captain. 'It was one of the most enjoyable periods I've ever had at a football club,' McAnuff adds.

Ross Embleton, like McAnuff, could see that momentum was building. With ten games of 2017/18 left, he was already looking towards the next campaign.

'Before every game, our changing room was wild. It was noise, music, people pumped up. And I remember standing there, in the huddle, ten games to go and saying, "Boys, if we can start building slowly and getting results, this will eat into next season. And when we come back, we'll be ready to fly.'

Taking off

On 9 June, the squad flew off for their pre-season training camp in Albufeira, Portugal. It was to prove a defining part of Justin Edinburgh's first full campaign.

New signing James Alabi is tasked with filming the squad behind the scenes. It's a sweet, almost innocent vlog, a snapshot of a team comfortable in their own skin, enjoying each other's company. A young Shad Ogie mucks about with an equally youthful Ruel Sotiriou, players on the edge of the squad but very much part of it all. Jobi McAnuff drinks from a two-litre bottle of water as his team-mates set up a game of *NBA*. He's happy making excuses about being 36 and having two young kids and not being able to play video games. He'll still have a go. Defender Joe Widdowson is invited to say hello to the audience watching on YouTube. 'Wag'wan YouTube channel,' he replies.

In another video, the manager talks of a 'spirit within the group. It gives us an opportunity' he says.

McAnuff was already revelling in his new role as club captain under the Portuguese sun.

'I thrive when people give me responsibility and Justin gave me that. In terms of giving me the captaincy, allowing me to lead how I felt was right for the group. And listen, in any successful group, the leader is not one person. But you're the one who has to set the temperature.'

Part of McAnuff's role as captain was to let the boss know how the squad was feeling, and on occasion, push back on his demands.

'He was old-school,' says McAnuff. 'And when I say old-school, it wasn't anywhere near the old school like we used

CHAPTER 10

to do pre-season. It wasn't just running for the sake of it. It would always be ball-related, and he would take guidance from the fitness coaches. But pre-season, you're working incredibly hard. It's a tough time. And we'd done a couple of the sessions and the lads were feeling it. I was feeling it.'

With a double morning and afternoon session coming up, the team asked their captain to have a word.

'I said, "Look, Gaffer, just letting you know, a few of the senior lads have come to me ... and you know, it's been a real tough few days. The running we're going to do in the afternoon, can we bowl it on to the morning and then have an afternoon where we can just chill, like get our feet up, and get ready for the next day?" And he just looked at me.'

Edinburgh wasn't happy.

'He went, "It's fucking pre-season. It's supposed to be hard. You are supposed to be tired. So go and tell the fucking boys, get themselves ready for this afternoon." But, to his credit, he tailored the session, so it wasn't as intense. That was his way of going, "I'm the boss. But I am going to listen." He respected the fact I'd come to see him, and it was a genuine bit of feedback from the lads. But that really set the tone for that season, because we knew that was the level we needed to get to. We've always got to do more.'

Vice-chairman Kent Teague also made the trip. Wearing a red Orient polo, black baseball cap and dark Ray-Bans, he can be seen hiding from the sun in a small gazebo with Martin Ling. They watch as Edinburgh oversees a training session on a sunburnt grass pitch, sand filling in where chunks of turf should be on the surface.

For Teague, this trip sets up the season.

'I had a conversation with Justin. We were sitting just out by the pool. It was the first time I'd really spent extended time with Justin. I had breakfast with Justin, lunch with Justin, dinner with Justin, drinks with Justin, out with Justin, in with Justin. Because when I went to pre-season, I would get up and I did *everything* all day with them and *everything* all night with them.

'And the thing that I said to Justin was, "The difference between the way we finished last season and us getting promoted is probably three per cent or four per cent. That's all. We're not far off. Now, the question is, what is the three per cent or four per cent for you, for your coaching staff, and for each individual player?" He built a plan for himself and each player that showed a five per cent improvement.'

Teague is proud of his role. Like the squad and coaching staff, he knows where he fits into the system. He knows what impact his own three-to-five per cent improvement can make.

'My role in life is to provide fundamental frameworks on which people can build greatness. So, my job is to help them understand the foundational or fundamental principles, and the frameworks on which they can build great companies, great lives, great relationships, great whatever they want to build. My job as chairman or vice-chairman, whether it's at a company, in my family, or at Leyton Orient, is to remind people of the foundational principles. That's my role.'

But it's not his only role, 'The other one is I'm the balancer. When everybody's super high, I'm tempering expectations. When everybody's super low, I'm cheerleading people up. I'm the moderator. And that's really valuable, because what moderation allows for, and causes, is long-term success.'

Just as Cryptic Kent promised a year previously on Twitter, 'Ours will be an example of winning consistently over long periods of time. Commitment is key.'

It was time to commit.

CHAPTER 10

The class of Leyton Orient
Saturday, 4 August 2018, Peninsula Stadium

Salford City 1 Leyton Orient 1

Before Ryan Reynolds had even looked where Wrexham was on the map, there was Salford City.

In 2014, a consortium of former Manchester United players bought their local non-league club. The 'Class of '92' – Gary Neville, Phil Neville, Ryan Giggs, Nicky Butt, Paul Scholes (and later, their fellow class member, David Beckham) – took ownership of Salford City, overseeing a meteoric rise through the divisions. Three promotions in four seasons saw Salford rise from the Northern Premier League Division One North – the eighth tier of English football, to the National League, one promotion away from the EFL.

Like Wrexham a couple of years later, Salford were the subject of a high-profile documentary, initially broadcast on the BBC and then on Sky. This broadcast publicity, plus their famous owners, alongside a couple of high-profile FA Cup campaigns, ensured that the media focus was firmly on Salford as they started their first season in the National League. For many bookies and pundits, they were favourites for promotion to the EFL for the first time in their history. They were the non-league team everybody was looking out for. And only two teams would be promoted: the champions and the winner of the play-offs.

Justin Edinburgh had ambitions of his own, of course. It was fitting that his Leyton Orient team would open the 2018/19 season away at Salford.

'It's been a rapid rise for Salford over the years,' said Edinburgh before the match. 'And I'm sure they'll be looking to continue that. They're a lot of people's favourites ... But I always believe it's about us.'

Andy Gilson, preparing for another season on commentary duties, was well aware of the threat Salford posed to Orient's promotion hopes.

'They [Salford's owners] threw a lot of money at the club,' he says. 'We were in a position where if it was a car race, you've got a Formula One car and the rest of us are sitting there in a Kia.'

The game is chosen to be broadcast live on BT Sport, a 12.30pm kick-off on a warm, sunny day in Salford. For the Class of '92 and BT Sport, it was a dream start. Just after half-time Salford take the lead, new signing Rory Gaffney coolly volleying into the Orient net past goalkeeper Dean Brill. It stays 1-0 for most of the second half, Orient pushing for an equaliser, hitting the woodwork twice and having a ball cleared off the line. Finally, in the 86th minute, the breakthrough comes – Orient's Craig Clay getting on the end of a knockdown from a corner, whipping the ball across the box, the ball deflecting into the net via Salford captain Liam Hogan.

Keren Harrison celebrated the last-ditch equaliser behind the goal with the rest of Orient's travelling fans. 'You feel your heart going,' she says. 'And then it's that big release of screaming. You just knew it was going to happen. It was always going to happen.'

With a battling late goal, Orient save an opening-day point against the league's most-fancied and famous team. Speaking afterwards, Edinburgh sums it up, 'We had to dig deep. I thought we showed great resilience, strength and character to come away with a well-earned point. Testament to the players. They never, ever, give in.'

The equaliser was the first of many last-minute goals. He could have been summing up the entire season.

CHAPTER 10

Mad as a box of frogs
Saturday, 1 September 2018, Proact Stadium, Chesterfield

Chesterfield 0 Leyton Orient 1

They don't let Kent Teague in the stands at Brisbane Road. He's too excitable. As passionate as any lifelong supporter, he's been known to excitedly smash computer monitors while streaming Orient games from his home in Texas. When he's in the stands, you can see why. He doesn't hide his emotions. Nothing is safe. Kent Teague in the South Stand at Brisbane Road is a genuine security risk.

When he goes to away grounds it's a different story.

'It's like, "Hey, you're on your own," he explains. He can do what he wants.

Teague was a gift for *The Sun*'s Dream Team series, *Love Of The Game*. A YouTube documentary profiling Orient fans, players and staff, it followed the club as the 2018/19 season progressed. In one clip, talking about his appearances at matches, Keren Harrison asks her son what he thinks of their vice-chairman. 'Mad as a box of frogs?' she suggests, affectionately. Footage from the series shows Kent on the gallery at Brisbane Road, falling to the floor at a chance missed, running around, pumping his fist as the team go into a 2-0 lead. Jumping on Matt Porter and Martin Ling who have stood to celebrate the goal, he does the same with regular fans in a clip from an away match, screaming 'get in there!' he's mobbed like one of their own.

Teague put the work in to be a fan favourite. The previous season had seen him in the country every six weeks, staying at the Lion and Key hotel on Leyton High Road for his ten-day visits.

'I wanted to be able to walk to the stadium, hang out at the stadium,' he says. 'Be with everybody, go to the training ground, all of that. It's really easy to get to the training ground from Leyton station. You just go up to Buckhurst Hill.'

The contrast with the previous ownership couldn't be starker. Francesco Becchetti had been living in a £20m mansion in Mayfair. Teague was living in a hotel off the High Street in Leyton, jumping on the Central line to Chigwell.

An investor, fully invested and passionate about his new project, Teague couldn't hide his passion as he walked back to his hotel after games.

'I can't tell you the number of times I would walk back to the Lion and Key and literally yell the entire time. I'm sure the people that lived down that road hated it after matches because I would literally yell how mad I was or how excited I was. I would yell the whole way.'

Teague couldn't be in the country as much in the 2018/19 season, but Dream Team had chosen a great year to follow the Orient. Justin Edinburgh's team moved into September unbeaten in seven games. Momentum was building. Expectations were rising. Then along came an away trip to Chesterfield with Teague in the away end. He made the most of his visit.

The game is goalless for 78 minutes before a high cross is looped in from Joe Widdowson. A Chesterfield central defender gets a head on the ball, clearing it from the attentions of substitute striker Matt Harrold and Orient centre-back Charlie Lee who has made a dash towards the box. The clearance is far from convincing, dropping down just behind the penalty spot. It bounces once, hanging in the air invitingly for the onrushing James Dayton to manoeuvre his body into the perfect position and rifle a blistering left-foot shot into the top corner of the Chesterfield goal. It's a beautiful strike. Just as Orient need it.

Teague, in among it with the fans, can't control his joy.

CHAPTER 10

'I call him "Daytes" – James Dayton, and I have a very clear memory of being at the angle where I could see where the ball just curved right into the top corner. I was like, "Do you want some more of that?! You want some more of that?! Is that what you want?! You want some more of that?!" You know, just going crazy. I was so excited.'

Everyone was. Maybe this was the season to get excited again.

11

Leyton Orient are breaking records in the National League.

By September, Orient are freely scoring goals and winning games. They beat local rivals Barnet 3-1 at home, defeat Harrogate 3-0 away and put five goals past Braintree in another away victory. They are 13 games unbeaten since the start of the season. It's a new club record, leaving Orient top of the league on 29 points, two clear of rivals Salford. The first defeat of the campaign doesn't come until the end of September, with a 1-0 loss at home to Sutton.

Over the next two months, the Orient express stays on the rails and pushes back to top of the National League.

The team won't lose another game until December.

Being the big fish

Justin Edinburgh hit the nail on the head.

'The last two, three, four years, this club was used to losing,' he said. 'And not only losing but being relegated. So, to turn that around as quickly as we have is a huge testament … congratulations to the players.'

He is, as ever, cautious and considered, but there's no denying it. Thanks to Edinburgh's leadership, Leyton Orient have learned to win again in the space of just a few months.

CHAPTER 11

'He was building his own side,' says Andy Gilson. 'He was getting the players in that he wanted, not what he inherited. And he also did make the point that we weren't that far away. He won the players over and they were reciprocal to his instructions. It was as simple as that. They did what he asked them to do. That's the secret of any successful manager, isn't it?'

And once again, Leyton Orient were scoring goals.

'We'd never been a free-scoring side,' continues Andy. 'But all of a sudden, we were burying teams. We expected to go and win, which was something that had been sucked out of the club for the previous four or five years. Everyone expected us to win more than we'd lose.'

It's easy to enjoy football when your team is winning. For fans like Keren Harrison, it was fun to be a Leyton Orient supporter again.

'What I really liked about the National League was being the big fish,' she says. 'We would go to all these new grounds that we would never get to go to. Clubs that would never end up being in the first or second round proper of the FA Cup. Getting to all these new grounds, being the big fish, turning up, the away end is full. We're all singing. Being in that away end was amazing.'

One away game stands out for Keren, a 3-1 victory at AFC Fylde. 'I really liked Fylde,' she explains. 'Because we took some cups home for washing up ... these sort of plastic pint pots.'

Printed on the side of the pilfered takeaway glasses, AFC Fylde had outlined their ambition: to be in the Football League by 2022. 'We always joke when we have a drink out of one of the cups,' she says. 'Oh, you know, Fylde didn't quite make it.'

They didn't. But Orient were getting closer. Two goals in the last four minutes (Bonne and Brophy) away at Wrexham at the end of November saw the Os enter December unbeaten away from home, and three points clear at the top of the league. A year after his appointment, Edinburgh was named National League Manager of the Month.

By the end of the year, Orient were still top of the league after an away draw with Dover. Speaking at the time, Edinburgh reflected on how far the team had come.

'It's been a brilliant year for this football club. We haven't ended it with the win we wanted, but let's look at how much things have changed and how much the players have achieved. It was a good point on the face of things, no side is going to win every week, there's going to be ups and downs along the way. We have come far in such a short space of time and 2019 is hopefully just the start of things to come.'

Then, at the start of January, Orient lost 3-0 to the Class of 92's Salford City.

Getting caught with your pants down
Saturday, 5 January 2019, Brisbane Road
Leyton Orient 0 Salford 3

This was not how Justin Edinburgh imagined starting the year. After hanging on for a 1-0 victory against Dagenham & Redbridge on New Year's Day, top of the table Leyton Orient faced third-placed Salford at Brisbane Road.

Within ten minutes, Orient are two goals down.

'What a start from the visitors,' says Andy Gilson, commentating for the Orient live stream. 'Two headers, two goals.'

Both the goals have come within the space of two minutes. A third comes in the 81st minute, a second of the match for Salford's Carl Piergianni ('He always causes a problem,' says Andy), and by the end of the game it is Salford who look like champions in waiting. It is a comprehensive defeat.

'They looked a very organised side,' says Andy, reflecting on Salford's performance. 'It was one of those occasions where we were caught with our pants down and absolutely brushed aside.'

Two weeks later and their pants are still down away at Ebbsfleet United. A comfortable 2-0 victory for the hosts leaves Orient looking over their shoulder. The title is now a three-horse race between Orient, Solihull Moors and Salford, with only goal difference and a point separating the three teams. Wrexham are also in the mix.

'We didn't compete well enough,' said Edinburgh after the Ebbsfleet defeat, which meant successive reverses for the first time in the campaign. Orient needed to bounce back quickly.

'You're going to get the odd hiccup and the odd bad result,' says Andy. 'It's a character-building curve.'

January finishes with a victory over Maidenhead and a pitch invasion by a squirrel, before cup commitments get in the way of February fixtures. But after a draw with Hartlepool and a 1-0 defeat at home to Maidenhead, Orient slip to third in the league.

Only the champions qualify for promotion automatically. Edinburgh and his team had work to do.

'I thought Barry Galvin was going to kiss me'

It is around this time that Edinburgh's leadership once again made a difference.

'I remember one game when it was getting really tight,' says Jobi McAnuff. 'We were in the dressing room, and he just came in. As soon as he comes in, everyone is all eyes on the gaffer. He said, "Listen, everyone's talking about the end, whether we're going to get promoted or not, but whatever happens, just go out and play and give me absolutely everything you've got. Don't worry about tomorrow. Don't worry about two weeks. Don't worry about the end of the month. If you just give me everything you've got, we will get promoted. I'm going to guarantee you that because we've got the quality.'"

For McAnuff, it was just another example of Edinburgh's rare ability to connect with his players.

'He just demanded absolute maximum effort, maximum focus and application,' he says. 'And the reason he was able to do that was because he was acutely aware that we had a life outside of football. He was fantastic at learning about you, whether someone's got a young kid, whether they are living away from home … He gave us that respect and understood what went into making a good footballer.'

Over the next two months, the team rewarded Edinburgh's trust and respect with performances on the pitch. March saw Orient battle away at Barrow, travelling the 300 miles to the Cumbrian coast on a Tuesday night for a 2-1 win. Then, there was a victory over promotion-chasing Wrexham (minus Ryan Reynolds) live on BT Sport, before 'a world-class save' from Dean Brill ensured an away victory over Aldershot.

Going into April, back on top of the league, Orient continued to fight. The 94th-minute equaliser against Halifax from Matt Harrold, the 'ginger Pelé', earned the Os another crucial point ('I scored one of the best goals of my career from about 12 centimetres') and there were 'absolute scenes' in the gantry as Orient won their crucial game in hand at home to Eastleigh. 'I thought Barry Galvin was going to kiss me,' said co-commentator Charlie Lee.

Brisbane Road was beginning to believe. Justin Edinburgh's team could do it.

With four games to go, the title was Orient's to lose.

CHAPTER 11

'What the hell is he doing?!'
Saturday, 13 April 2019, Gander Green Lane
Sutton United 1 Leyton Orient 2

'It was a game of incredible incidents,' said Justin Edinburgh. In many ways, it is a game that defined the season.

Leyton Orient made the short trip to Sutton United sitting top of the league, two points clear of Salford City and four clear of Solihull. If Orient could win again, it would keep them in the top spot with only three more games to play. The chasing pack are running out of matches.

It's a glorious sunny day in south London for the travelling Orient fans who have packed out the terraces behind the goal and are spilling into the corner of the stadium at Gander Green Lane. There's nerves, but excitement. This is a game they need to win.

For Andy Gilson on commentary duties once again, the day is not going to plan.

'The whole day for me was an absolute nightmare, an absolute nightmare. I probably commentated on, I don't know, 800, 900 football matches. That was probably my worst ever commentary, just dreadful. Everything went wrong.'

As the teams make their way on to the pitch, Orient in their red strip, Sutton in all yellow, Andy tries to find the right words. He is only just catching his breath.

'We got a train from Clacton that got up to London,' he says. 'And there was a fire on the line somewhere. So, when we got out at Sutton, I had to run to the stadium, which was about a mile and a half, two miles. I got there with about 15 minutes to spare. I asked the media manager if I could have a co-commentator and he refused. And I literally had moments until they came out on to the pitch.'

For a game of 'incredible incidents', the first half is largely incident-free. At half-time it is still 0-0. The biggest talking point is that Sutton have swapped their goalkeeper, Jamie Butler. He is replaced by Ross Warner, a key part of the Sutton team who made the fifth round of that season's FA Cup, beating Leeds United in the fourth round. Nobody knows it yet, but he will play a key role in the outcome of the afternoon's match.

Andy is still so distracted during the break that he missed it completely.

'I didn't realise that at half-time they changed the goalkeeper. I didn't hear it being announced. I just didn't notice. Somebody actually texted me and said, "I don't think you realise he's been changed!" I was trying to do the [other] scores at the same time. And I repeated the same phrase, I think, two or three times.'

The phrase Andy kept saying was 'the only shot in anger'. He explains that repeating the same phrase is a 'cardinal sin' for a commentator. And people noticed. 'Somebody put it on the internet,' he says. 'And it was a disaster. Absolute disaster.'

While Andy is dealing with his troubles in the gantry, Orient are struggling with their own down on the pitch. Young forward Jonah Ayunga has put Sutton ahead in the 52nd minute. 'It's a screamer … absolutely no chance for Dean Brill,' says Andy in his commentary.

Dan Happe, playing left-back for Orient that day, remembers the team's reaction on the field. 'You look around, don't you?' he says. 'You look around at your team and you go, "Well, we've got to do something here." We knew what we had to do. Just try and dig it out and get a result.'

It is Happe who gets Orient back in the game. In the 64th minute he rises above the Sutton defence and puts the ball into the back of the net from a Josh Koroma free kick. It is a lovely looking header that doesn't actually hit his head. 'I scored off my shoulder,' he says. 'It was a sense of relief, like, "Come on. Let's go again."'

CHAPTER 11

Ten minutes later, everyone is talking about 'an incident'. Substitute James Dayton, who has been troubled by injuries all season, goes down after a strong challenge from Sutton's Jonathan Barden. It is a season-ending injury.

'It was a terrible challenge,' recalls Andy. 'The poor fellow had problems with injuries, and you could see the frustration there. He's going to miss out on the last games as well. It was tough on James. He'd always given his best to the club.'

To make things worse, the referee doesn't even caution Barden. Instead, Dayton reacts. With his ankle already swelling, he rips off his boot as he is sat on the ground before throwing it into the pitch in frustration. His boot bounces, skimming across the playing surface in the direction of the referee. The official isn't happy.

'If he threw it at the ref, it wouldn't surprise me,' says Happe. 'We didn't actually ask him afterwards, because he was just in pure pain at the time.'

Speaking after the match, Justin Edinburgh can't believe what he's seen.

'I'm not criticising the ref for not blowing up, he allowed us to play on, but he's got to understand. The boy has got a serious injury and he's thrown his boot on the floor in frustration.'

It gets worse. As the Orient medical team are removing Dayton from the pitch on a stretcher, the referee reaches for his pocket and shows the injured player a red card. 'That is ridiculous,' says Andy on commentary. With 16 minutes to go, Orient are down to ten men. With Salford leading 3-0 and Solihull getting an equaliser against Havant & Waterlooville, Orient need another last-ditch comeback of their own.

As the minutes tick by, Sutton push for a winner, but Brill stands firm in goal. With a couple of minutes left, news comes in from the West Midlands, 'Solihull have taken the lead in stoppage time,' says Andy, just as the Sutton full-back passes the ball to Warner.

The scorelines leave Orient level with Salford and just one point clear of Solihull who they will face in the penultimate game of the season.

Then it happens.

As the ball rolls back to Warner, the substitute goalkeeper flicks it up, presumably to give himself an easy volley to clear, but he loses control. 'There's a mistake at the back!' shouts Andy, as the ball spins off behind Warner, deep in the Sutton penalty box. 'What the hell? What the hell is he doing?' thinks Gilson, just as Macauley Bonne sprints on to the ball, touching it away from the stricken Warner who can't help but take the striker out, clattering him to the floor. The referee immediately points to the penalty spot.

'It's the clearest image,' says Happe. 'The keeper just started juggling the ball. It was like fate. Everything that happened was just meant to happen.'

Bonne steps up and makes no mistake in front of the travelling Orient supporters, coolly slotting his penalty past Ross Warner for his 23rd league goal of the season. He runs to the corner, mobbed by both fans and players.

'I looked down at the Orient fans below me, below the gantry,' says Andy. 'And they were just going absolutely potty. And you just *knew*. You just *knew*.'

Matt Porter was also at the game.

'When McCauley scored that penalty at Sutton ... there's a video of me celebrating on Twitter. I left that day and I thought, "We're back. We've done it." That was the single biggest moment [of the season].'

After eight minutes of added time, the referee blows the final whistle. The win keeps Orient two points clear of Salford and three ahead of Solihull at the top of the table.

CHAPTER 11

For Dan Happe and the Orient players, they know they are nearly there.

'Just incredible scenes when it went in,' he says. 'And in the changing room, unbelievable. It was like – it's actually going to happen.'

Just three games to go.

'This is where I belong!'
Monday, 22 April 2019, ARMCO Arena
Solihull Moors 0 Leyton Orient 0

The Os beat Harrogate at home on Good Friday, live on BT Sport once again. 'Lift-off at Brisbane Road!' says the commentator as Josh Coulson puts his team 1-0 up after only two minutes. Ninety minutes later, Matt Harrold finally makes sure of the three points, his header from a corner securing his fourth goal of the season. All of his goals had come in the 90th minute or later – another example of Justin Edinburgh's team playing until the very end.

Harrogate are pushing for a play-off place themselves, looking to get in the EFL for the first time in their history. It was another big win. 'We're at the top, every game's a big game,' reflected Coulson in his post-match interview.

The victory leaves Orient two-points clear of Salford and three ahead of Solihull, with only two games left of the season. With a far superior goal difference, the title is in the Os' hands. It could be decided at their trip to Solihull on Easter Monday. Salford need to lose, Orient need to win. Of course, a defeat could take things out of Orient's hands.

I watched the game on BT Sport, looking after my 18-month-old daughter in the garden. A glorious spring day, I nervously watched, juggling a just-about-walking child and a sun-dappled laptop while one of the biggest away days in Orient's history unfolded.

Alongside many others, Billy Herring made the trip with his dad, joining the Orient fans who had found the makeshift bar behind the away end. A local celebrity supporter had made the trip from Essex as well.

'I remember being in the marquee just singing songs with Gatsby [Liam 'Gatsby' Blackwell] from *Towie*, which was just really weird,' says Billy. 'And everyone was just in such a good mood. It was celebratory. I think everyone felt confident because we were playing well. Everyone was absolutely buzzing, getting to the ground and seeing the team bus pull up and everyone saying hello to the players getting off. We didn't stop singing the whole game. We absolutely took over that whole ground.'

It is an attritional match, tight and cagey at times and it is the home team who come closest to getting a goal. Deep into the second half, substitute Jermaine Hylton fires a close-range shot towards goal only for Dean Brill to block and then smother on the floor. A few seconds later, Coulson bends down to gratefully hug him around the back as the Orient keeper cradles the ball safely in his arms.

'That was massive,' recalls Matt Porter. 'It was a goalmouth scramble. That was a massive save.'

'It was a really tough place to go,' remembers Dan Happe. 'They were all like six-foot-plus. They were absolute bullies, but we handled it so well.'

Another massive moment comes with just a few minutes to go as Solihull defender Kyle Storer finds himself unmarked with a free header at the back post. The Orient fans watch on with relief as he directs his effort wide, the ball slipping safely past the post. After 91 minutes the referee blows his whistle, the game ending goalless. All eyes turn to Salford.

'It was proper backs-to-the-wall, a proper grind-out,' remembers Billy, who was waiting nervously with the rest of

CHAPTER 11

the Orient fans for the result of the Salford match to filter through. Playing AFC Fylde at home, Salford had gone 1-0 down in the first half. If the scoreline stayed the same, it would mean Orient only need a point to secure the title on the final day of the season.

In the middle of the pitch, Happe and Brill are being interviewed by BT Sport. 'They're still going though at the Peninsular Stadium, Salford desperately seeking an equaliser,' says the presenter. A few seconds later, a massive roar erupts from the away support. Salford have lost. Orient are one game away from promotion, and with their superior goal difference, even if they lose it would leave Salford needing to win by six goals to overtake them.

'The job's almost done?' asks the BT Sport presenter.

'Not yet,' says Brill. 'It's close ... next week, hopefully it'll be our day.'

Behind them, the Orient fans already believe. 'We are going up, say we are going up,' they sing.

'I have never seen a crowd like that day,' remembers Ross Embleton. 'People were possessed. I remember looking at people in the crowd and thinking, "I know this geezer. He just looks out of control!" This means so much to everyone.'

Kent Teague is also in the crowd after joining the away fans in the stands at half-time.

'I go to matches and I wear my suit,' he explains. 'And at half-time, it's like Superman takes off his costume. And I'm walking through the away fans and they're clapping me. And I remember taking off my tie and taking off my coat and becoming one of them. And oh my God, it was crazy when we drew, and we found out that Salford had lost. Our fans are going fucking nuts. I was in the stands cheering. The players saw me in there. Justin saw me in there. He was like, "What the hell are you doing up there?" And I'm like, "This is where I belong!"'

As Teague celebrates, surrounded by sweating fans swinging their shirts around their heads, one man remains calm among the excitement. As the team coach leaves, Billy Herring joins the supporters applauding the squad off. He remembers getting a word in with Justin Edinburgh. 'Justin, we've done it. We've done it,' he says. Edinburgh doesn't agree. 'Not yet,' he replies.

Not yet, but nearly. Not even Orient could throw this away. Could they?

This is how it feels
Saturday, 27 April 2019, Brisbane Road
Leyton Orient 0 Braintree 0

On a cloudy and grey day, the storm of the past five years is finally lifted. It is done in the most boring way possible.

Salford are losing. Solihull can't win. All Orient need is a draw. And Braintree are already relegated.

Not that everyone is relaxed.

'It wasn't out of the realms of possibility for us to get beat by Braintree,' says Billy Herring. 'Even though they were getting relegated. Because that's just what Orient do. But when we heard that Salford were getting beat, all the nerves just kind of went.'

'It was a funny game,' says Paul Levy, who watched from his usual seat in the South Stand. 'It was an anticlimax, and it wasn't sunny. I was like, "Is that it? Is that what it feels like to win the league?"'

But nobody cares. Braintree don't offer much and neither do Orient. The players take a pragmatic approach. A team who Justin Edinburgh had taught to win, mature enough to play for a draw.

'A draw was good enough,' continues Paul. 'And that's what we played for. You can't suddenly make the players *not*

CHAPTER 11

nervous about losing a game at home that could potentially have won them the league if they had just played for a draw. You've got to play it safe sometimes. Completely on board with that. But from a footballing spectacle, it was terrible.'

'We were actually really bad in that game,' remembers Dan Happe. 'It was one of those ones where everyone thought, "We've done it. Let's just get past this game." The mindset was *after* the game, not *in* the game.'

On the bench, Ross Embleton is struggling to enjoy the occasion.

'I remember with about five minutes to go, a guy came down and leant over that little silly rope they have next to the dugout, and he patted me on the back, and he went, "We've done it, mate. We've done it." And I went, "No, we haven't. No, we haven't. It's five minutes left." I was still convinced that Salford were going to score eight. I am in the Orient dugout and we're about to win a league. I just sat there, and I was like, "This just is the most surreal feeling ever."'

Finally, the referee blows his whistle for full time. Leyton Orient are champions.

'Everyone was going crazy,' continues Embleton. 'But I just remember walking around the edge of the pitch. I didn't know what to do. I wanted to run into the crowd. I wanted to run to the family. There's a video my daughter took of me at the final whistle. I just sort of walk on to the pitch. I sort of clap my hands. I'm just lost. I still, to this day, can't explain what that was all about.'

As the fans and substitutes invade the pitch on the final whistle, Jobi McAnuff finds himself in the middle of it all. The returning hero, the man Justin Edinburgh had made his captain, finally, after the failure and pain of his previous time at the club, he has achieved what he set out to achieve. The mass of supporters on the pitch lift McAnuff up, placing him on their shoulders. Their captain, a club legend for life. The image is captured by hundreds of smartphones, alongside the lenses of professional photographers. Everywhere you look, joy.

'That was probably the biggest positive,' he says. 'Yes, winning the league. But being able to walk away from that football club and actually have a fanbase who maybe thought a certain thing of me before, just sort of see me for what I am – that was the best thing about that.'

I ask him what it feels like, to be literally lifted in the air by adoring fans.

'It's a real tough one to articulate,' he says. 'There's so much going into the game. As much as we *know* we're going to do it that day, it still had to be done. And all of a sudden, you're quite literally riding a wave. You're up. You can now see all around you. You're on someone's shoulders. I'm just looking around. Everybody's chanting.'

The chanting doesn't stop. 'We are going up, say we are going up.' Over and over again. A refrain shouted from the guts. Repeated, en masse, looping around – the fans making it true, making it real. Leyton Orient have won the league. They are promoted. This can't be taken away.

'That is 100 per cent the big, big highlight of my career,' continues McAnuff. 'The scenes around it, the drama, the excitement, the emotion, the happiness. Just to be able to be a part of it in our own stadium, with all those fans that have been through all the shit times. In terms of that appreciation of doing something when you failed before, it definitely feels sweeter. You look back at some of the pictures, and they are moments that will live with me forever. There's no question about that. Just real special, special times.'

On the pitch alongside the players and hugging his fellow fans, Billy Herring can't contain his emotions.

'I absolutely cried my eyes out,' he says. 'It was such a relief. It was just great. We're back. Just relief. Absolute relief.'

CHAPTER 11

Two years earlier, these fans were on the pitch in protest. Today they are on the pitch in celebration. United and jubilant, only one Orient.

For fans who had been at both matches like Billy it is special. For a player who had been there for both occasions it is just the same. Dan Happe was in the stands for the protest in 2017, a young player who'd been with the club since the age of 14. A man who had played in that final League Two season with the other young squad members. He was there at the Colchester protest. He knew what it meant to the club. Now, he is on the same pitch having just won the league with his team. Like the rest of the players, he is mobbed by the fans.

'That felt amazing,' he says. 'For me, being there for both, it was definitely a sense of relief. We're back where we belong, back in the EFL. I didn't know at the time, but I was celebrating like no other. The contrast was unbelievable. The vibe was mad. It was crazy. Just getting promoted was ... you can't actually describe what it's like.'

On the bench, kit manager Ada Martin is doing his own thing.

'It was bedlam,' he says. 'But I remember just picking up coats and putting them on the bench. It was quite surreal. Really, really strange. Everyone was hugging each other. And all I could think about was just tidying up the bench. And then it hits home and you run around and start acting like an idiot.'

Up in the gallery, Kent Teague is taking it all in.

'I remember standing up on the owner's balcony. And it still gives me goosebumps. And it does make me cry sometimes when I think about it. Because we had just won. We had just been promoted. We drew 0-0 and they started singing, "Kent Teague, he's one of our own." And they sang that a lot that day. The singing was phenomenal.'

Teague eventually finds himself pitchside. A few weeks earlier, during a BT Sport interview, the crew had tried to persuade him to stand on the pitch for a better shot. Teague refused.

'I said, "No, I can't go over that line. I won't go over that line." I never stepped on to the pitch the first two seasons. And to this day I will not step on. I have a hard time even stepping on the training pitch! They're like, "What is wrong with you? I'm like, "That's your spot. This is mine. I can be over here."

'It is the thing that is really important to me. I give respect to other people for the clear talent and skill that they've developed. "This is where you live. This is where you work. This is where you are. This is your space." I have a crazy amount of respect, so much respect for your space, your talent, your skills, your abilities, your work, that I will not step on there.'

The metaphorical as well as physical contrast with the previous ownership is almost too perfect.

'I will never forget asking Justin, "Can I?" And the look on his face of just pure joy, saying, "I'm so glad to say, finally, yes, you deserve to step over!"'

'I also have a reverence for the pitch,' adds Teague. 'There are certain things that truly are sacred, that are given to us by God. I know this is a little weird, but that hallowed ground to me *is* hallowed ground. It means a lot to me what we accomplish on that pitch.'

It means a lot to everyone.

In the dressing room, Justin Edinburgh is giving the speech of his life.

'Enjoy tonight, and tomorrow, and Monday…'

The party in the home changing room is already in full swing when Justin Edinburgh walks in.

CHAPTER 11

'We've celebrated on the pitch, champagne flying everywhere,' remembers Dan Happe. 'Gone into the changing room, carried on the party. The speaker's gone on straightaway. Everyone's jumping in the air, champagne all over, dripping from the ceiling. It was filthy in there, puddles in the changing room. And he [Edinburgh] comes in, still having a party, and he goes, "Everyone sit down, sit down, sit down."'

Edinburgh has already embraced Jobi McAnuff. A long hug, full of joy, he lifts his captain up, clutching his face, before they both join in with the rest of the players jumping around, singing in celebration.

Once everyone has sat down, Edinburgh stands to address his team.

'I'll just say that it's been an honour to lead this group – players, staff, and the board of directors and everyone connected to the football club. For me, when I come in here, this club was going one way. That was into the Conference South. So, credit to you, because there's not been a lot of change ... Remember, enjoy tonight, and tomorrow, and Monday, and Tuesday, and Wednesday ... And when we get down that airport!'

At this point Edinburgh is jumping around, arms out like he's already flying the plane to Marbella. The players roar in excitement, running towards him, champagne spraying once more.

'Everyone's got a smile from ear to ear,' says Happe. 'And then we went on holiday for four days. It was just an absolute party the whole time.'

For Martin Ling, it is an extra special day. His son, Sam Ling, had been a key part of the team that year.

'That's probably my best achievement in football,' Martin tells me. 'But that's added with my own boy playing in the team. Winning a game to go in the Premier League and all that … Nothing gave me the same thrill of seeing the team go up with Sam as part of the squad. You can't beat that.'

Meanwhile, in the Leyton Orient supporters' club, a special guest has arrived.

The trophy had been paraded around the boardroom – staff and players getting their opportunity to have their photos taken alongside the cup with their families. But Kent Teague knew he needed to share this experience with the fans. 'I said to Nigel [Travis], "I'm taking the trophy with me into the supporters' club."' After a hastily arranged security escort, he headed downstairs and made his way next door.

'I'll never forget the look on the fans' faces when I walked in with the trophy,' he says. 'For them to be able to be with it, that was huge. Because none of them, or very few of them, had ever seen a championship trophy. They'd never had their picture taken with the championship trophy. And just the joy that was in the room that night.'

As she always is, Keren Harrison is in the supporters' club, at the heart of the celebrations. I asked her what it was like.

'Mayhem,' she says. 'We had been warned that it was coming. So, we had tried to keep a little area clear. I burst into tears when I held it. It was as if everything that had gone before was irrelevant. All the hard work was for this. We'd backed the boys, and that was my way of thinking, "Well, actually, the boys backed us." This is the boys' way of saying, "Thank you for backing us." It was emotional.'

Ross Embleton recalls walking down the tunnel and seeing some of the lads from the Orient academy, a part of the club that carries a special significance for him. He started his football career as a player in Leyton Orient's centre of excellence and by his mid-20s he was the coach running the academy.

'I thought, "Oh my God, we've just kept these kids in academy football." We'd have lost the academy if we hadn't been promoted that season. It was just surreal. I didn't even go out that night. Everyone else, all the other staff, all went to some bar in Billericay. I just stayed at the club until God knows what time, in the same kit, covered in champagne.'

'You never forget what it felt like,' says Paul Levy. 'Getting involved with all the jubilations and celebrations and the players being driven up and down Leyton High Road. It was brilliant. I stayed around for a bit on the pitch and got invited up to the boardroom to lift the trophy, to meet Justin. It was lovely.'

The party had only just started.

'All I could see was pounds, pounds, pounds!'
Sunday, 19 May 2019, Wembley Stadium, FA Trophy Final

Leyton Orient 0 AFC Fylde 1

There was one last day of the 2019 season to enjoy.

Three weeks later, Leyton Orient played AFC Fylde in the FA Trophy Final. Almost five years to the day after the 2014 play-off final, Orient once again walked out at Wembley. This time the team are competing for the non-league cup, attempting to secure a non-league double.

Around 23,000 Orient fans make the trip across London. Orient are back.

'I remember being really amazed at how many people we brought,' says Kent Teague. 'I can't tell you the number of times that I will meet someone in London and they're like, "Leyton Orient! You know, they're the second team I check." And I always say to them, "Hey, I appreciate the fact that

Leyton Orient is your little brother or your little sister team. I love that. I appreciate you.'"

Despite having to sit down throughout the match ('I remember how stodgy it was. I wasn't allowed to stand. I had to watch my mouth, all that!'), Teague enjoyed his day out at the home of English football. 'It was great. My mom and dad came. You know, my family was there. I had a lot of friends that flew in from the United States. And it was just a great day.'

Symbolically it was a great day for Teague and the rest of the Orient fanbase, despite the result.

A Danny Rowe free kick in the 60th minute secured a 1-0 victory for AFC Fylde, but Orient had plenty of chances to win it.

Jordan Maguire-Drew managed to hit Matt Harrold instead of an open goal from five yards. The same player had earlier hit the post from a free kick, while Marvin Ekpiteta headed a corner on to the opposite post. Full-back Joe Widdowson also hit the same post after a skilful run and a shot that looked destined to squeeze into the bottom corner of the net.

Teague had mixed feelings about that particular strike.

'I told Joe that if he scored at Wembley, I would write him a cheque. Actually, I wouldn't write him a cheque, I'd give him cash. I was going to give him £10,000 in cash. After the match, Joe walks up to me and he goes, "All I could see was pounds, pounds, pounds. I couldn't even see the goal. You fucked me up, man!"'

A disappointed Justin Edinburgh in the post-match press conference praised his players and the whole club.

'I'm proud of the football club, I'm proud of my players. They've been incredible all season. And the fans again today. The numbers that we've been backed by. It's quite incredible. You know, we accomplished the goal; to get back into the

CHAPTER 11

Football League ... The lads are hurting, but they have to take a lot of credit for the season they've had.'

The final question posed to Edinburgh is a simple one, 'Looking ahead to next season, what do you think can be achieved?'

It is an easy answer.

'Well, we don't want to go there and make the numbers up. We need to take momentum forward. I think we're equipped for that off the pitch ... I think everything's in place.'

It was. Everything was in place.

Then the inspirational manager suffered a cardiac arrest.

12

'Can you throw anything else at this club?'

Matt Porter, June 2019

'Thank you for being you'
Saturday, 8 June 2019, Barclaycard Arena, Hamburg, Germany

As chief executive of the World Darts Corporation, Matt Porter was attending to his day job at the World Cup of Darts. In the post since 2008, he'd already grown darts into the giant sporting brand it is today.

'I remember taking the call in the car park from Nigel [Travis],' he says.

A week earlier, he had taken another call.

'Nigel phoned me and said, "I need to tell you something. Can you talk? Justin's in hospital. He's had a cardiac arrest." I thought a cardiac arrest was a heart attack. I didn't know there were different things. I said, "Is he OK?" He said he might not be OK. He might not get better. And I thought, "Oh, yes he will."'

On 3 June, Justin had been in the gym. Aged 49, a former professional footballer, he was full of life and energy, riding high on the extraordinary triumph of his team. Nobody expected him to go into sudden cardiac arrest. With no defibrillator on site, he was rushed to Basildon University Hospital where he fought for his life.

CHAPTER 12

'I never believed he'd die. I lost my mum when I was quite young,' says Porter. 'I've sort of tuned in with tragedy, if you know what I mean? But I still couldn't imagine it. I mean, a young, fit man who had just been so successful. And we got on so well with him. "This can't happen. This can't happen now."'

In contrast, Kent Teague was expecting the worst as soon as Travis called delivering the news that their manager was in a coma.

'I asked Nigel right then. I said, "Chances that he comes out?" Nigel's like, "Five per cent." Well then, I'm going to go say goodbye to Justin right now,' recalls Teague.

For the next few days, everyone associated with the club was hoping for good news. Like most regular fans, Matt Simpson wasn't aware of the severity of the situation.

'I don't think, to begin with, we knew how serious it was. I wasn't thinking that [Justin dying] was a possibility at that point. There just wasn't that much information. Obviously, it was quite serious. But, I didn't *know*.'

Porter, in constant contact with Travis, was realigning expectations every day. Trying to process what might happen. Hoping for the best.

'Right, he might wake up, but he might be in a wheelchair, or he might take two years to learn to walk again. And as every day passed, you were thinking, oh, that won't be too bad. Two years, then he can walk again. It'll be all right.'

But it wasn't. Porter took that call from Travis in the car park of Hamburg's Barclaycard Arena. Justin Edinburgh had died.

'Can you throw anything else at this club?' thought Porter, in despair.

For a fan like Matt Simpson, the news hit him harder than he could have imagined.

'When a celebrity I don't know dies, I'm not one of those people who feel that deeply. I can respect the loss to their family and friends and respect the loss to their art or whatever, but I don't feel like I'm genuinely grieving or generally upset about those sort of things. But with Justin Edinburgh … I *really* felt that. I've never met him, but your football club's really important to you. And my season ticket during those days was right behind the dugout. I was always close to him. I felt just deeply sad about it. Firstly, because he's a relatively young guy and left his family and friends, but also just for what he could have achieved at Orient. The loss of what could have been.'

What could have been? For Matt, for everyone, this was supposed to be the start of something.

'We never got to see what would happen. He probably would still be our manager. He was really good. I suspect he would have done well in League Two, and we'd have got promoted after two or three seasons. I think he was great.'

For Teague, as much as he mentally prepared himself to let Justin go when Travis first called, he still hangs on to his memory in the most 21st-century of ways.

'I will give you a little insight into something that nobody knows. On my phone, even though I just got a new iPhone, at the bottom of my text messages, it says, "Justin Edinburgh, 5/30/19." And his last message to me was, "Thanks Kent." And when I click into it, I have all kinds of messages from Justin. And I have never deleted them, and I probably never will.'

For a young player like Dan Happe, Edinburgh's death hit him hard.

'It was really difficult,' he says. 'The last time I saw him was when we went back to the Marriott, Waltham Abbey after the [FA Trophy] final. It was a special moment. Everyone, all my family, all his family. We're all on the dancefloor, just having a good time, just celebrating the season. And then we had our summer holidays. Everyone goes away. I've gone away for my dad's stag do. I'm meant to be in this good spirit celebrating my dad. And then I get a message that he's passed away. And I'm just destroyed. It was an absolute tragedy. No one could believe it. It was really tough. It was really hard for me.'

Supporter liaison officer Keren Harrison was also celebrating before she heard the news.

'I was at a friend's party,' she says. 'It was in the garden, and I just threw my drink in the bushes. I just ordered a taxi, went to the station, went up by train, and got some flowers on the way. That was a numbing day. It was very strange. You're grieving like it's an aunt or an uncle or something, because you see them every week. You probably see them more than you do an aunt or uncle. You don't know them personally, but you *know* them. They're a big part of your life. It's a horrible, strange feeling.'

People still struggle to express their feelings. The sudden death of their football team's manager at such a young age couldn't be prepared for.

On the night the news was announced, Matt Porter took to social media. In a long, emotional post, he managed to find the right words.

'We adored him and his impact on us all was profound … I sit here with tears in my eyes on the night he left us and I can't even begin to understand why this has happened. Justin, to be able to call you a friend was a privilege. To be able to have been with you on our journey was a dream and to honour your memory will be our way of keeping you with us. Rest in peace Justin, and thank you for being you.'

What *is* an Orient?

Justin Edinburgh's death changed everyone's life.

We met Mark Hannah earlier. He's the actor who moved to London from Edinburgh in 2019, training at the London

Academy of Music and Dramatic Art, looking for a new football team to follow. He walked into the supporters' club at Leyton Orient and that was it. He's an O. But why did he choose Orient in the first place?

'It remains the most visceral example of fate I've ever experienced, borderline supernatural, utterly incredible.'

I'm talking to Mark via a video call from his parents' house in Edinburgh. When we speak he's about to start rehearsals for a touring show in Scotland and is back home for a couple of months. One of several Scottish Os (the saltire pops up at many an away game), Mark's story is unique. It's intrinsically tied up with Justin Edinburgh as well as famous actor and Orient fan Daniel Mays.

'It actually started as far back as 2017. I was doing a project at the Royal Court Theatre and I was cutting about central London. I had some time to kill before I had to go there for a rehearsal. And I was walking past Goodge Street Station, and Danny Mays was walking directly towards me.'

If you think you don't know Daniel Mays, you do. He's been in *everything*, although more specifically *Line of Duty*, *Ashes to Ashes* and *The Long Shadow*, as well as several films including *Rogue One* and the remake of *Dad's Army*. He'd also spent some time at the Royal Court Theatre when he was younger. And he's a lifelong Orient supporter.

'We got chatting about all sorts. And he was like, "Are you going to apply to drama school? You totally should."'

Mark took Mays's advice and ran with it, getting into drama school a few months later. He tweeted Mays, who congratulated him, and they started chatting over social media.

'This was 2017, at the height of Becchetti and I initially made a mistake. I said, "Oh, you support West Ham, do you not?" And I was humbled! Orient is one of those names that you hear on Sky Sports News or *Gillette Soccer Saturday* or whatever. And you're like, that's a strange name. I wonder what that name is. What *is* an Orient? There's a mystique about it.'

Around this time, content creators Copa90 released a 15-minute video on their YouTube channel. *Riots and Relegation: What the f*** happened to Leyton Orient* documents the last few games of the 2017 season. Mark remembers being deeply moved by it.

'That video was just so powerful. I thought, oh, this poor club. And I vaguely kept an eye on the first season in the National League. And in 2019, on the 8th of June specifically, which was the day that Justin Edinburgh passed away, I had my final recall at the London Academy of Music and Dramatic Art. And that's a full eight hours. One of the most intense days I've ever experienced. As I was walking away I looked at my phone, and the newsfeed was exploding, the club announcing that Justin Edinburgh had passed.'

Among the tributes and messages posted across social media over the next few days, Mark saw a message from Daniel Mays, 'Utterly shocked and saddened at the passing of our manager Justin Edinburgh. Words aren't enough. He will be remembered as an Orient legend. Our saviour who made us believe and dream again.'

Two weeks later, Mark found out he'd been accepted into the London Academy of Music and Dramatic Art. His life was going to change.

'That team Danny spoke about in the street, and then all this stuff that's happened since, even the guy's surname … I've never met a Scottish person with the surname Edinburgh. It's an English guy from Essex. I thought, that is absolutely bizarre. And that mystique of that word *Orient*, I'm like, wow, it could only be them, surely. I felt so bad for them because of the rollercoaster, the brink of financial obliteration, then going back into the Football League and then losing the manager only weeks after that.'

Tragically for Mark and his friends and family, his sympathy for Leyton Orient very quickly became empathy.

'Just over a month after Justin Edinburgh had died, one of my very close childhood friends was killed in a car accident. He'd fallen asleep at the wheel. I was ready for my life to change, but not as heavily or as drastically as that. I had to have something outside of the training that was going to consume my life. I thought, fuck it. I don't know anything about this club. I don't know anyone there. I don't know where the ground is. Don't know where Leyton is. But it was a calling. These people are going to help me grieve, because we're going to do it together.

'I didn't believe in fate prior to that. But I really, really do now. All of these things happened within about four weeks of each other. It was just ridiculous. I'm not just choosing that club. It's something much higher. I'm not a religious man, but there's a force there that said, "You are going to come here and it's going to be fine. It's going to be class." Which is exactly what it was.'

As Mark and Orient grieved, the club had a new season to prepare for. The team were back in the EFL. But they didn't have a manager.

'It's still difficult to grasp what has happened'

The memorial service took place on Tuesday, 16 July at 11am. A sunny day, players arrived in black suits and sunglasses, fans stood outside, shielding their eyes from the sun and breaking into spontaneous applause. A line-up of former Spurs stars including Glenn Hoddle, Teddy Sheringham, Sol Campbell and Les Ferdinand joined what the order of service described as a 'Celebration Service for the life of Justin Edinburgh'. As the ITV news report at the time described, 'It was a service

CHAPTER 12

filled with music. Songs from the gospel choir echoed around the cathedral grounds and friends and family shared their happy memories.'

Jobi McAnuff spoke to the congregation. He naturally fits his role as captain, leading the team and striking the right tone on the day. Speaking to ITV, there's a hint, an awareness, that the reality of Edinburgh's death hasn't been fully processed, 'The family made a point of wanting it to be upbeat, and very much celebratory. I think the tone of it was hit perfectly. Obviously, it's still difficult to grasp what has happened.'

And there was so much to do. There was no time to grieve. The new season started in under three weeks. Everyone just had to get on with it. As Matt Porter says, 'You had no choice. You had to deal with it because the league wasn't going to wait for us. No one was going to say, "Well, just take your time, Orient. Let us know when you're ready to start playing again." We had to be ready to go.'

Kent Teague was trying to deal with the situation from across the Atlantic. He regrets not being closer.

'It was very tough for all of us. And I'm managing it from afar. I should have flown in. But I didn't. I can't remember why. I should have just told my wife, "I got to go to London," and I should have been there.'

It wasn't just the geographical distance that made things extra hard for Teague. The uniqueness of the situation was isolating too.

'Here's the first thought that goes through my head, "I need to go find a reference of someone else that's been through this as an owner so I can ask them how to handle it." But it's never happened before. We couldn't find an owner who'd had a manager or head coach pass away within a month of winning a championship. Never happened before in history. So now Nigel and I are just making shit up. Fundamentally, I know the steps to grieving, the psychological, the sociological, all that. But sometimes it's really hard to put principles into action when your thinking is so clouded. And that's what happens in grief.'

The cloud of confusion and grief affected everything. There were the unexpected off-field arrangements; what do you do with all the flowers and cards left by fans? Should they build a statue? Should they name a stand after Edinburgh? Who gets invited to the funeral? As Teague says, 'It's a thousand decisions and it's a football club. So, guess what? People are going to disagree with us no matter what we do.'

Despite the challenges and the grief, the whole club had no choice. They had to step up. They had to face the crisis head-on. None more so than Edinburgh's former assistant, the new interim manager, Ross Embleton.

'It will ruin your career'

On 19 June, just three days after Justin Edinburgh's memorial service, Leyton Orient named Ross Embleton as interim head coach. He had exactly two weeks to prepare for the first game of the season.

Eleven days earlier, alongside Nigel Travis, Kent Teague, Martin Ling and senior players Craig Clay and Josh Coulson, Embleton had been in Boston preparing for life back in League Two. The show needed to go on.

The group, minus Embleton, were sitting around discussing how to move forward. At the time, in the immediate aftermath of the news, everything else felt more important than who was going to manage a football team. But somebody needed to do it. Leyton Orient's grieving players needed a leader before a permanent manager could be found.

'I walked into the conversation,' says Embleton. 'And I just sat on the end and didn't get involved. I wasn't part of it. And then I just went, "I'll do it."'

CHAPTER 12

It made perfect sense. As Embleton told the team at the time, 'I know the scenario. I know the players. I know the situation. I've been part of the recent history. And when you're ready to put a manager in, you can just take me away. I don't want to be a manager.'

Looking back, Embleton reflects on the importance of a heated conversation he'd had with Nigel Travis over dinner one night, 'Me and Nigel had a real intense conversation about performance and results in sport. My argument was you never achieve results consistently unless you get performance. And Nigel was like, "Yeah, but it's all about the result on the Saturday." We both agreed with each other, but we had different angles of approach in the conversation. And we *really* went at it over the table. It was brilliant.'

For the leadership team, Embleton's attitude and his ability to hold his own with the chairman was a major factor in proving he could do the job. His coaching ability had always been well respected by the staff and senior players, but his 'intense conversation' with Travis did him no harm as well.

'"I think you've just passed your interview,"' Embleton recalls Ling saying. '"You said you're happy to step up. And you've shown strength to go with the chairman and talk to him on a level. Not many people would do that."'

With Embleton in place, Teague and the leadership team started the search for a new permanent manager.

'My advice to every person who contacted us and said they wanted to be the head coach was, "You don't want to be the head coach." I said, "It will ruin your career. You cannot follow Justin Edinburgh. He's now become a saint. He won a championship. He was a saviour. You'll never get near him."'

Embleton, meanwhile, got on with the task of leading the team into the 2019/20 season. With players arriving back in London at different times after their summer breaks, each one deserving one-to-one chats and as much help processing the situation as possible, the period of mourning lasted for weeks. The work began to take its toll.

'Every day, I'd wake up and I'd be like, "Oh my God, I've got to go and do this again,"' Embleton tells me. '"I've got to go and mourn again."

'And then one day, we got all the boys into the stadium, and I just said, "Look, I'm going to be the one that you all look at at some stage and think I don't care, but I've got to show you something else. So, while we're all mourning, I will be too, and I'll have my moments, but you won't see it because someone's got to try to put a football team together. And I'll be that someone.'

The emotion of the situation could hit the squad at any time. Embleton recalls going into the changing room at half-time during the pre-season matches having to comfort his players. 'There was boys in tears,' he says. 'Just another moment for someone.'

As Martin Ling said to the BBC at the time, 'It has been a period which I have never, ever faced in my football career. You don't get a manual to deal with it, but you deal with it the best way you can deal with it, with Justin always in your thoughts.'

'Every pre-season game,' continues Embleton. 'For the right reasons, everyone wanted to do a minute of applause or a minute of silence. So, we had that build-up all the time. The emotion was just so much for everybody to cope with. And once we got into the season, I started to get people come up to me saying, "I think we need to move on now." And I'd be like, "You don't know the half of it. You don't know the half of how everybody is and how everyone's feeling."'

On 3 August 2019, an emotionally drained Ross Embleton led Leyton Orient out at Brisbane Road for the first game of the League Two season.

CHAPTER 12

As he walked out of the tunnel he remembers thinking one thing, 'I'm fucked.'

Tears on the balcony
Saturday, 3 August 2019, Brisbane Road
Leyton Orient 1 Cheltenham Town 0

Leyton Orient won that first game of the season. An emotional day at Brisbane Road saw Josh Wright, Justin Edinburgh's final signing, score the winner in a 1-0 victory. As he scored, he pointed to the sky and ran towards the gallery in the main stand. Charlie Edinburgh, Justin's son, later posted on social media, 'There were some tears on the balcony when that one went in.'

There were tears all around that day.

I was in the East Stand packed in with some friends, peering round the old columns that hold up the roof to watch the match. The atmosphere was charged. Ross Embleton describes the extent of the emotion before the game as 'just ridiculous'.

Sensing that the players needed as long as possible to compose themselves after the minute's silence, Embleton ran on to the pitch before kick-off.

'I got the starting 11 into a huddle, because there were tears and emotion. And I thought, "If I do this, at least it gives them another minute or two to regain themselves." I remember looking around and just saying, "Listen, I ain't going to say nothing, but I'm just trying to give you all a minute to settle."'

It did the job. Leyton Orient got their opening day victory. The team and the club weren't ready to move on, but at least they were moving. And after 13 games, Embleton's team were just about mid-table, five points off the play-offs. It was a solid foundation for any new manager to build on.

Then, on 16 October 2019, the club announced Carl Fletcher, the former Plymouth Argyle manager and ex-Wales international, as their new permanent head coach.

He lasted less than a month.

'Carl Fletcher was stunningly sacked by Leyton Orient after just 29 days,' screamed the *Evening Standard* on 15 November, citing senior players and staff voicing concerns about his management. There was a cultural misfit and Leyton Orient had made a mistake. Nigel Travis acted quickly.

'We screwed up,' he told talkSPORT at the time. 'Carl did not screw up, we screwed up. We do not blame him, we blame ourselves.'

'I think Carl Fletcher was probably just too risky an appointment,' Matt Porter tells me. 'But it comes down to where we were as a club at that time. We weren't quite as strong or as recovered as we thought we might have been.'

Orient weren't ready to move on. The players and staff needed someone they could trust, someone they knew.

Martin Ling, with the benefit of hindsight, can see why the appointment didn't work.

'It was near enough impossible,' Ling says. 'He [Fletcher] found the situation in the club difficult because it was like a stranger coming into a group. It's like a stepdad coming into a marriage and you're the kids. It wasn't just the football. It just didn't feel right. It didn't fit. And then Ross took it again.'

Even before Fletcher was appointed, Travis had consulted senior players and staff on who they thought was the right man for the job. They all said Embleton was the man to take Orient forward. But Embleton didn't want the permanent job. He recalls speaking to Travis over dinner one night.

'"Nigel, I don't want to do it,"' he said. '"It's not me. I've said to you from the beginning, I'm happy to step aside and let someone new come in. It's not what I want to do."'

But this time he accepted, signing a 12-month rolling

CHAPTER 12

contract early in the new year. 'I didn't do the job with my arm up my back,' says Embleton. 'I don't want anyone to think that. But what I did start to feel was if I didn't do it or didn't take it, what was going to happen? Because they had already made a managerial appointment that hadn't worked out. And then it started to make me think, "Well, actually, if I don't step in and do this, where do I end up?" The club would've been well within their rights to bring someone in and say, "Let's clear the decks and move on completely."'

Embleton describes the way his appointment was announced, 'I actually got announced as manager about 12 hours before I was supposed to. I obviously knew I was getting the job the next morning. It had all been agreed and signed. And I was sitting on the bike in the gym and Lingy phoned me and he was like, "Mate, have you got a minute? Has your phone just gone mad? I said, "As it happens, yeah."'

The announcement was live on social media, an administrative error robbing Embleton of his time in the spotlight.

'My big moment, holding the Leyton Orient scarf, Leyton Orient permanent manager, and it got announced while I was sitting on a bike in the gym at Chigwell!' he laughs, rueing his misfortune.

For the new head coach, it was just the start of the bad luck that was to follow. And the start of a breakdown in relationships that went well beyond football.

'I remember speaking to Ross in Boston,' recalls Martin Ling. 'And saying to him, "You know, one day I'm going to have to sack you? Because it doesn't matter what happens, that's my job. The only way it doesn't happen is if you're really, really successful, and then you go to a bigger job."'

Like the Germans winning on penalties, Ling's words are one of football's certainties, 'One day, I'm going to have to sack you.'

13

By March 2020, Ross Embleton's Leyton Orient are sat mid-table in League Two. After a 2-1 home win over Cambridge United, the team are 17th in the league. They are on a run of seven games undefeated at home, 12 points clear of the relegation zone.

As Embleton prepares his team for the upcoming trip to Bradford, the Premier League and the EFL make an announcement. Due to the Covid-19 pandemic, professional football is to be suspended until 3 April 2020 at the earliest.

By May it is confirmed that the remainder of the season will be cancelled. Swindon Town, under young manager Richie Wellens, are confirmed as League Two champions.

Leyton Orient don't play a professional match again until September.

When the 2020/21 season finally kicks off, football is played behind closed doors until December 2020 when a small number of fans are allowed back into stadiums under strict controls. Apart from the lucky few, matches can only be watched through streaming services.

A third national lockdown comes into effect in January 2021, banishing supporters from the stands once again. Despite a 2-0 away defeat to Bolton Wanderers at the end of the month, Leyton Orient sit in tenth position, just four points from the play-offs.

CHAPTER 13

'Watching shit lower-league football'

Speaking to the people involved – players, coaches, staff and fans – they all say the same thing. Covid denied them something. Whether it was their matchday routine with their family or friends, the opportunity to play against Premier League opposition in the EFL Cup, or the chance to celebrate a stunning comeback with supporters in the stands, Covid turned the beautiful game into a tedious pastime.

For supporters like Matt Simpson, streaming matches was the only option.

'It was the least interested I've ever been in Orient,' he says. 'I still watched them all, and I still wanted us to win. And I still sort of punched the air if we scored. But I felt the least engaged I ever have, because you take away everything around the experience of football. I love the ritual. Saturday three o'clock just feels so traditional. I still go with my dad. He's 86. My nephew comes, my two daughters alternate week to week. It's a three-generation family thing. The experience of going to Orient is what's important to me. It's not the only thing that's important – I love us winning, but it's an important part. With all of that stripped away, it just became watching shit lower-league football.'

For the players, being a footballer came with its own unique challenges.

'You had to train on your own for a long time,' Dan Happe tells me. 'Just running on your own. It wasn't a nice place for a footballer, but it wasn't a nice place for anyone. You just had to get on with it. Everyone was going through the same thing. I still had all my family back home, but it wasn't nice to get football ripped away from you just like that.'

Nigel Travis ensured the players and full-time staff were paid in full, despite no matches being played for six months. But when football, minus the fans, returned in September 2021 things didn't feel right for the Leyton Orient staff.

'The first month was really strange,' Ada Martin tells me. 'Playing football and there's not a soul in the ground. It was the most tedious season going. It really was. It just felt pretty pointless that we carry on playing. People still can't leave the house. We're going to hotels for overnights where we couldn't eat food because they didn't have kitchens working. It was the strangest thing.'

As kit manager, Ada had the added pressure of ensuring everything he did was completely by the book and in line with the ever-changing Covid guidelines.

'Nigel was big on it,' he says. 'The Football League were very big on it to the point where if you break the rules, they could deduct your points. I couldn't wash training kit. We weren't allowed into the training ground. We had to erect marquees in the car park. At one time we were having three tests a day. It was ridiculous. Two coaches going to away games. Fourteen people per coach, single hotel rooms. It must have cost the clubs fortunes. You just got fed up with it in the end.'

Director Matt Porter was one of the privileged few allowed to watch matches throughout the whole period. For a time, it was a novelty.

'I learned so much about football watching games during Covid. And you can hear everything. You can hear the referees. You can hear the players. It was just bizarre. I actually quite enjoyed it. After a while though, that novelty wore off.'

The period was particularly tough on head coach Ross Embleton.

'I feel like I really missed out from not having the Orient crowd at games,' he says. 'We'd done some really good things during that Covid period, and it felt like that couldn't get recognised because no one was around.'

Three key moments stand out for Embleton: the EFL Cup second round defeat of Plymouth, where striker Danny

CHAPTER 13

Johnson scored a last-minute winner for the Os; the emphatic 4-0 home victory over Bolton in the league in October; and the cruelly forfeited EFL Cup third round fixture with Premier League giants Tottenham Hotspur. Joy and memories, like so much around Covid, simply stripped away.

'I could have managed against José Mourinho,' says Embleton. 'I could have taken my Orient team at home to play against Tottenham. And I never got to do it. I had so much given to me in terms of getting the opportunity to manage my football club. And then I had such massive moments that I couldn't celebrate. There were so many really good things that we didn't get to enjoy and build together.'

Things got worse. By February 2021, a slump in form saw Orient slip to 14th in League Two. And after seven games without a win, Martin Ling's words came true.

He had to sack Ross Embleton.

A photo of the corner flag

'I loved him like a younger brother,' says Martin Ling. 'It was the hardest decision we had to make.'

Embleton and Ling had worked together for years. When Ling was Orient manager in the mid-2000s he appointed a young Embleton to run the academy, helping to guide his career before taking him on as his assistant when he became manager of Swindon Town. Embleton lived with Ling in the West County, he was there to support him during his illness, and he was the first person Ling phoned when he needed trusted staff to come and rebuild Leyton Orient.

It was a partnership that spanned decades and stretched beyond the purely professional.

'Incredibly close,' is how Embleton describes their relationship. One particular moment from his time as Orient head coach epitomises their affection. It took place before a home game at Brisbane Road.

'I used to hate being in the changing room before the game when the boys were out warming up,' says Embleton. 'So, I went upstairs to do a Q&A with the people on level three [the hospitality punters]. I walked in and Martin was being interviewed. I was waiting to do my bit and I heard him say, "This boy's got every opportunity, every chance to be good at this, he loves this club, I look upon him as another son." That meant an unbelievable amount.'

You don't often hear about the personal side of football, the human side. The modern game is far more progressive with mental health and general human empathy than it ever has been, but there's still a coldness to football that people live with. Managers, players, staff – they know that at any moment they could lose their jobs. They must detach themselves from feelings, from caring too much. It's a harsh reality of the industry. And it's one of the reasons that Embleton never wanted to be the permanent manager of Leyton Orient in the first place.

'I knew my time was going to come to an end probably a little bit quicker than most other people,' he tells me. His position as established coach, rather than established and proven manager, was always something he felt was against him. 'I had three draws and four defeats in seven games, and I was gone. I always felt like I was an average run away from getting the sack, whereas most other people have to have a total car crash to get the sack.'

Ling describes the day he sacked Embleton as 'awful'. For Leyton Orient's director of football it 'scarred what was a beautiful relationship into being not as beautiful as it was before'.

For Embleton, it was equally painful.

'I felt like I'd served the purpose,' he says. 'I think that I got myself and the club to the point where everyone felt we were ready to move on. And I knew it was coming.'

CHAPTER 13

The moment came in late February after a 3-1 home defeat to promotion-chasing Tranmere.

'We went a couple of goals down and I said to the staff, "Listen, there's half an hour to go. I'm just going to do what I want with the team because I'm getting the sack after the game." And they were like, "That'd be stupid. We're not in that sort of state." And I said, "No, no, listen, I'm getting the sack. It's fine. I'm just going to have a go at this."'

As Embleton walked down the tunnel after the match, the usual greeting party of Ling, Matt Porter and CEO Danny Macklin weren't there. Ling then made his way to the changing room to deliver the news.

'Ross was walking out of the changing room and he said to me, "If it's going to be now, give me the decency so I can go and say goodbye to my players." I said, "Well, it's now. We're going to sack you."'

Embleton recalls the exchange, 'I just said, "Look, I don't want to go away and have to phone people up and do all the cringey text messages and phone calls. Let's just do it like adults." And I think it's probably my only regret, really. That was the only conversation I really had with anyone about me leaving. No one really sat me down and said thanks for everything.

'You get over it in time. It's just very, very difficult. Mine and Martin's relationship had broken down. And the biggest thing that still hurts me is the amount of relationships I lost becoming the manager. Relationships mean everything to me.

'I'd had moments with all of that squad in success. Then a contrast of emotions with what happened with Justin. To lose all of that, just didn't make sense to me. When people say, "Oh, that's football," – none of that was football. The success part was, but the other emotional stuff, that's got nothing to do with football.'

But football, like life, is cruel at times. Despite the club's affection for Ross Embleton, the announcement went out on social media with the image that always accompanies a managerial sacking.

As Embleton says, 'I got the corner flag photo.'

14

Jobi McAnuff is appointed interim head coach to replace Ross Embleton, with Orient still chasing the play-offs. The club finish the season in 11th, 12 points adrift of the final play-off place. McAnuff leaves his role in the summer and announces his retirement as a professional footballer.

The bulk of the squad who won promotion from the National League are released in the close-season. 'It was just a natural end to a cycle,' says McAnuff.

Leyton Orient start 2021/22 with 11 new signings.

And a new manager.

The Day of the Jackett

It was a fresh start. A new team with the same goal: to get promoted to League One as soon as possible. As Orient entered the fifth season of the six-year plan, there was a feeling that this could be the year. And on 21 May 2021, the signing of a proven, big-name manager sent ripples of excitement throughout the club.

Kenny Jackett was a marquee managerial appointment. A serial promotion-winner, he had led Swansea back into League One before gaining promotion to the Championship with both Wolverhampton Wanderers and Millwall. He'd even taken Millwall to an FA Cup semi-final at Wembley.

This was it.

'I see Leyton Orient as a club full of potential,' he said at the time. 'That's the attraction. My own personal ambition is to take us to the next level.'

Jackett was one of three candidates interviewed by Martin Ling and the recruitment team. He was a standout name from the beginning.

'We ended up taking Kenny for the job,' says Ling. 'Which looked an absolute perfect picture. Everyone telling me how clever I am. "This club is able to pull a rabbit out of the hat. We've got Kenny Jackett!" And when I remember the interview process, his knowledge on our players and the players in the league was sensational.'

Fan and podcaster Paul Levy was convinced Jackett was the right man.

'I didn't even need to think about it,' he says. 'The pedigree, where he's coached, what he's achieved, what he'd done in football. To have someone of his stature come on board to take a little Leyton Orient back to where it needs to be was frighteningly brilliant. And he signed some technically really good players.'

The new names coming into the club over the summer felt like another exciting step forward. Paul Smyth, the Northern Ireland international blessed with lightning pace, joined from QPR; veteran former Premier League midfielder Darren Pratley joined after his surprising release from Charlton Athletic; skilful full-back Tom James was snapped up on a free transfer from Hibernian. They were joined by more promising players looking for a home: Omar Beckles from Crewe, Aaron Drinan from Ipswich, Harry Smith from Northampton and on-loan winger Theo Archibald from Lincoln.

And the squad hit the ground running.

A comfortable 3-1 victory away at Joey Barton's Bristol Rovers saw fan Mark Hannah (you remember him) knock

CHAPTER 14

himself out while celebrating an Archibald strike from outside the area. When he emerged from hospital in Bristol later that evening, Orient were second in the league and starting to dream.

'The first three months were amazing,' says Ling, but in reality, the first five were positive. Two 4-1 home victories, against Sutton United and Swindon Town in November and December were the icing on the cake. With Harry Smith and Aaron Drinan combining up front, Jackett's team were sitting in the play-off positions by early December, looking to kick on over Christmas. However, a few days after the Swindon victory, Orient lost 2-1 at home to Crawley Town. The defeat was frustrating, but the injury to Tom James, excelling at wing-back, was to define the season. He was ruled out for three to four months with a hamstring injury.

New captain Pratley, who had worked under Jackett at Swansea, reflects on this period. Things weren't quite right.

'I don't think we had a real identity of how we were playing,' he says. 'There was no real game plan. It was a little bit off the cuff. I think we were winging it a little bit. That can only last for so long. And it caught up on us.'

After the comprehensive victory over Swindon in December 2021, Leyton Orient didn't win another league game until 19 March 2022.

Needless to say, Jackett was no longer the manager by that point. And Orient were once again looking down at the relegation zone.

Blood was shed this night
Tuesday, 22 February 2022, Brisbane Road
Leyton Orient 0 Bristol Rovers 2

As Tuesdays go, it was pretty awful. I'd met my brother after work and we decided to have a drink at Liverpool Street.

Plenty of time for a pint or two, then jump on the tube for the 7.45pm kick-off. Our mate had joined us, a fellow Orient fan who couldn't make the match. We discussed the recent horrible form: three defeats in a row, just two points since December, Orient suddenly looking over their shoulder at the relegation spots. Back in early December when the team had romped to that 4-1 victory over Swindon Town with a frantic performance under the Tuesday night lights, it left the fans bouncing away from Brisbane Road. Orient had been knocking on the door of the play-offs. This loss of form was troubling.

We probably stayed ten minutes longer than was sensible, but we still had plenty of time to make kick-off. As soon as we arrived on the tube platform we realised we'd be running to the ground. Severe delays on the Central line. A journey that should take 12 minutes was about to take, well, who knows how long.

It all felt appropriate for watching Orient at the start of 2022.

'We were on that really good run pre-Christmas, and we were due to play Bristol Rovers on New Year's Day,' remembers Matt Simpson. 'And they were on their coach, and they pulled out [due to Covid]. I love New Year's Day football. It's literally my favourite day to go and watch football. I always love it. And I was really annoyed that it got cancelled. But I felt there was something duplicitous about the way they had gone about it, given we were in such good form, and they weren't. For me, that was the turning point.'

It was. A Covid outbreak resulted in almost an entire month where no football was played. Orient never recovered.

Eventually the tube arrived, stopping at Leyton just as the rearranged match against Bristol Rovers was kicking off. We ran up the stairs from the underground and legged it down the high street. The match had already kicked off, so

CHAPTER 14

my brother decided to ease into some mad six-minute-mile jogging pace. The sort of pace nobody should attempt after a pint or two. I was wearing a backpack, a long Parka and some Dr. Martens. There was only one way this was going to end.

The past month had been horrible watching the Orient. Since football returned at the end of January, the team had played seven matches, losing five and drawing two. And the football had been awful. Aside from exactly one goal, the highlight of the year had been a fox running on the pitch during a 0-0 draw with Port Vale.

As we rounded the corner out of Coronation Gardens and on to Brisbane Road, the inevitable occurred. The pints, plus backpack, plus Parka, plus Dr. Martens boots, plus stupid running pace finally worked their magic, combining with a pavement curb to result in me completely stacking it. I slammed on to the road, knees first. My hands followed, immediately starting to bleed. My backpack flung up over my head as my arse pointed to the sky, a red Levi's tag flying gently in the wind. A red warning flag.

My brother helped me up and I looked down at my knees. Jeans torn, weeping blood, I hobbled into the ground. We were just in time to see Bristol score the first of their two goals. Another convincing defeat, a fourth loss in a row, the team only five points above the relegation zone.

Sitting on the train home, it was of no surprise when we checked Twitter to see that image again: the picture of the corner flag at Brisbane Road. The accompanying copy simply read, 'The Club can confirm that it has parted company with Manager Kenny Jackett with immediate effect.'

Blood was shed that night.

Once again, Orient needed a miracle.

15

'If you fuck this up, man ... we're going to look like fools.'
Kent Teague and fellow board member Nick Semaca, speaking to Richie Wellens, Autumn 2023

The second coming

Martin Ling had a saviour in mind. His name was Richie Wellens and he had just been sacked by Doncaster Rovers.

For Wellens, it was his second sacking of the year. Prior to Doncaster, he had taken the high-profile job as manager of Salford City, employed by Gary Neville and the Class of '92 to get Salford promoted into League One. In 2019 Salford had eventually joined Leyton Orient in League Two via the National League play-offs. Their ambitious owners were desperate to climb the divisions, and despite winning the EFL Trophy at Wembley and being only six points short of the play-off positions, Wellens had been ruthlessly fired within five months of his appointment. And the Sky TV cameras were there to capture it all.

It wasn't supposed to be like this.

A year earlier, Wellens had led Swindon Town to the Covid-hit League Two title. He had retired as a professional footballer just three years before. A former Manchester United youth team star, he had forged a successful playing career in the Championship and League One with teams including Blackpool, Doncaster Rovers and Leicester City. After his title victory with Swindon,

CHAPTER 15

he was seen as one of the most promising young managers in the country.

A year before Kenny Jackett's sacking, Ling had invited Wellens to interview for the vacant managerial position alongside Jackett. He was one of the final three Ling put forward to the board in the spring of 2021.

The problem was that Wellens already had another role on the table, at Doncaster.

'Within the first five minutes, he told me that he's 90 per cent sure he's got the Doncaster job,' says Ling. 'I said to him, "Why are you coming to have a coffee with me, then?" He said, "I want to see what the club's about, what you're about, and I don't think meeting people at your level is ever detrimental." That's smart. This is where I really liked him. And I went away and said that out of the three I'm putting forward, he's the one I like best.'

Ling knew Doncaster was a club close to Wellens's heart. Even as he tried to convince him to change his mind via a phone call, he knew it was a futile exercise. 'As I was going through it, I'm thinking, "I'm wasting my breath here." I said, "I wish you all the best, and look, our paths might cross again one day."'

It was late February 2022, in the wake of Jackett's sacking, when their paths crossed again. 'Richie's just got the sack [from Doncaster],' says Ling. 'And you just think, "Hmm, that's interesting. I really liked him."'

Ling didn't need another coffee with Wellens to put him forward to meet the rest of the hiring team. He quickly arranged an interview with Matt Porter, Nigel Travis and incoming CEO Mark Devlin.

Meeting for a three-hour discussion in a London hotel, they were immediately impressed.

'We decided that we'd really put him through his paces,' says Travis. 'And actually, one of the attractions to us was that

Richie had learned how difficult football management was the hard way. He left Oldham, Salford, and Doncaster under difficult circumstances. Swindon, where he had success, was different. And then he got hit by Covid. So, he had a lot of experiences on the rough side of football management. Then we obviously talked about how he approached different situations. "What happens if you're 2-1 up, or 2-1 down with ten minutes to go?" We really put him into a situational analysis. Within about an hour, I decided this was a goer.'

Travis has a HR background. He's interviewed a lot of candidates in his career. But for Travis, football managers are often some of the best prepared-people at an interview.

'They go and see the team several times,' he says. 'They stand with the fans. Listen to what the fans say. It is quite amazing how well-prepared they are, and they usually come with some form of presentation. We put Richie through that. We concluded that he was the guy. He was engaging, challenging. He was fun and he seemed very enthusiastic about the job.'

'I started to get the same vibe again,' adds Ling, reflecting on the conversations as they developed. 'He was just like Justin. You know what I mean? You can have a laugh. I can have a laugh. But he knows when to be serious. He knows how to manage.'

There was one last piece of due diligence to be done. Travis picked up the phone and called Wellens's former boss at Salford City, Gary Neville. 'He gave me some of Richie's high notes and low notes,' Travis says. 'And we decided to proceed.'

The club formally offered Wellens the job. But would he take it?

Barry Hearn celebrates on the way to victory over Peterborough United in the 2014 play-off semi-final. Leyton Orient was his folly, but he loved the club.

Chris Dagnal, moments after his missed penalty in the 2014 play-off final. In the background, Rotherham United celebrate. As Russell Slade said, 'Fine lines, isn't it?'

'He's got no hair, but we don't care.' Russell Slade salutes the travelling fans at Notts County, the match Becchetti told him he had to win to keep his job.

Francesco Becchetti displays his passion from the gallery at Brisbane Road.

'This is where I belong!' Kent Teague clenches his fists as he raises both arms in the stands away at Solihull Moors, on the way to the National League title in 2019.

Justin Edinburgh celebrates winning the National League on the final day of the 2019 season. 'There's no point in interviewing anyone else,' said Matt Porter when considering candidates for the role.

Owner Nigel Travis lifts the National League trophy with Justin Edinburgh. 'I've only got one goal,' he says. 'That Leyton Orient is thriving in 100 years' time.'

Camera phones and professional lenses capture the moment Jobi McAnuff lifts the National League trophy. Everywhere you look, joy.

'Another moment for someone.' A devastated Dean Brill lays his shirt in the dugout in memory of Justin Edinburgh, just weeks after his team celebrated winning the National League title.

'One day I'm going to have to sack you.' Covid turned football into a tedious pastime for many. Ross Embleton sends instructions to the team as Martin Ling and Matt Porter look on from the gallery.

'Like a dog with two dicks.' Richie Wellens plays to the crowd after victory over his former team, Salford City.

Orient's ecstatic players celebrate securing promotion away at Gillingham. The floodlights stay on so everyone can enjoy the moment. It was a 'totally Orient way to go up.'

George Moncur wraps up the 2022/23 season the way he had started it with a penalty in front of the South Stand. The 2-0 victory over Crewe secured the League Two title for Orient.

Paul Smyth lifts the League Two trophy. His goals were vital in Orient's success. Far left, captain Darren Pratley celebrates with two hands in the air.

16

March 2022. Despite the offer to Richie Wellens, Leyton Orient are still without a manager. Former National League-winning striker Matt Harrold, now a coach with the club, has been put in interim charge.

His first game is a home defeat to fellow strugglers Carlisle United. Orient end it with ten men after Theo Archibald is sent off, receiving two yellow cards in just three minutes. Three days later, Harrold takes his team away to local rivals Colchester United – also fighting for their league status. In the 93rd minute, Orient's young midfielder Ethan Coleman scores an equaliser, saving a point for the Os in a 2-2 draw.

As Harrold leads his team out for the visit of Stevenage the following Saturday, Leyton Orient sit in 18th place, just three points clear of the relegation zone. Watching from the stands at Brisbane Road are prospective manager Wellens and his assistant, former Orient midfielder Paul Terry.

The match is a drab affair. The crowd are restless. The football is poor. But once again, Harrold's team show some fight. This time Archibald, back from suspension, scores an equaliser in the 94th minute and the game finishes 2-2.

Richie Wellens is already on the motorway when the goal goes in.

'Why don't we go together? One, two, three ...'
The Redbridge roundabout, connecting the A12 to the M11, is just a few miles east of Brisbane Road. You can be there in just over ten minutes if you beat the traffic. And Richie Wellens has made good time.

Paul Terry is sat in the passenger seat, streaming the last few minutes of Orient's home tie with Stevenage on his phone. The pair had met while doing their UEFA A Licence coaching qualifications a few years earlier and it was a partnership that immediately hit it off. 'People on the course were asking how long we'd known each other,' says Terry. 'People thought we'd known each other for years.'

As Wellens pulls on to the M11, heading back north, the game at Brisbane Road enters additional time. Stevenage are still 2-1 up, having taken the lead in the 32nd minute. By the 75th minute, both Wellens and Terry had seen enough. The occasion hadn't done the job of convincing them to take on the role.

'The atmosphere in the stadium was dead,' recalls Wellens. 'The standard of the game was really, really poor. And when I was driving home, I was thinking, "You know what? I've just been let down by one club. Do I really want to throw myself into something that I'm not sure of?" And I was literally thinking that as Theo Archibald equalised.'

'We were talking,' adds Terry. '"There's a lot of work to be done ... I think they've got some good players ... what do we do?" And then Theo put one in the top corner, and I had to pull the car over because we went crazy.'

Terry describes it as being like that moment in *Only Fools and Horses* when Del and Rodney finally become millionaires,

CHAPTER 16

their three-wheel van rocking as the pair wildly celebrate by the side of the road. 'Do you want to go first or shall I?'

'Subconsciously, we were thinking, "What should we do?"' continues Terry. 'But when the goal went in, we just looked at each other ... "There's our answer. Let's just do it." It just reaffirmed it to us both. We realised it was definitely for us.'

They had streamed the previous match against Colchester as well; two last-minute equalisers in as many matches. '"So they've got character,"' Wellens remembers thinking. 'I thought, "OK, let's dig into the bottom of this." I just felt like there was good players. And I thought, "You know what? With a little bit of tweaking, a couple more quality players, we can do something here."'

With an offer on the table from the club, Wellens just had to give Martin Ling the nod and the job was his.

'I looked at Leyton Orient and I said, "These could be a top-half League One club. And at the moment, they're 20th in League Two. So, there's a lot of room for improvement." It just felt right,' Wellens said.

Four days later, Wellens was announced as the new manager of Leyton Orient.

And it just felt right.

Without realising it, Theo Archibald had scored one of the most important goals in the club's history.

'The best version of me'

Before Wembley 2014, there was Cardiff 2001. Richie Wellens was there. He was playing for Blackpool as they defeated Tommy Taylor's Leyton Orient in the Third Division play-off final. It was Orient's second play-off final defeat in two years; Blackpool were Wellens's first club after he left Manchester United.

'Very easy game, wasn't it?' he says, with a smile. 'I went on loan to Blackpool at the end of the previous season [from

United]. We got relegated. So, I thought it was right I try to stay and get us back up. And luckily, we got back, first time of asking.'

Now firmly wearing his Orient colours, I meet Wellens in the coaches' room at the club's Chigwell training ground. There's a large square table in the middle of the room. On the walls, movable magnetic tiles featuring the squad's fit and injured players sit beside the requisite dartboard.

We start by talking about the initial approach from Martin Ling, a man he first spoke to after his Swindon team tore Orient apart at Brisbane Road in September 2019.

'I probably had ten minutes with Lingy to myself. And I just liked him,' he tells me. 'You tend to speak to people, and straight away, you get a vibe off them if you like them or not. And I liked him.'

After the disappointment of his time at Doncaster ('It was just an impossible job') Wellens admits he needed a little time to reset before his next challenge. But when the next opportunity came along, he was ready.

'This was like a caged animal being let out. I've just been thrown under the bus. I wasn't given any opportunity to be successful at Doncaster. "Whoever gets me next will get the best version of me,"' he remembers thinking.

In the February of 2022, he was also in the running for the manager's position at former Premier League club Bradford City, who had been languishing in the lower divisions for the past two decades. Thankfully for Leyton Orient, Mark Hughes was offered the job, meaning Wellens could turn his attention to the Os. He spoke to his various contacts about the club. They told him everything he needed to know: Orient was a good club, with a fanbase starved of regular success.

He could tell that Kent Teague and Nigel Travis were good owners as well. 'They're really, really, top people,'

CHAPTER 16

he says. 'Total opposites. Really contagious people. And everybody likes Leyton Orient. You've got no other opposition supporters that really dislike them.'

As we talk, Paul Terry comes into the room. At the time of our interview, both Terry and Wellens still live in the north of England, Terry as far north as Durham. It meant that taking on the roles at Orient required sacrifices from the outset. 'We've got a culture here that there's no excuses,' says Wellens. 'Do we get tired at times? Yeah. Do we have to make sacrifices to our family? Yeah. But we signed up for it. So one thing we can't do is, we can't moan.'

Talking to Wellens, it's clear he has a burning desire to succeed. There's an infectious energy, focused on being the best he can be. Like his former boss Gary Neville, another man with a relentless drive to succeed, it all started at Manchester United. Playing for England under-17s to under-19s, with players who would go on to be superstars, Wellens was in the elite of young English footballers. However, his only senior appearance for Alex Ferguson's team came as a substitute in a League Cup defeat to Aston Villa. And as 'one of the best young players in the country' he should have done more.

'I never worked hard enough,' he says. 'Was never professional enough. Never worked on my body enough to be a Premier League player. I had a decent career, but I never fulfilled that talent I had. Every day I wake up with a tinge of guilt. So now I'm going to put the work in to become the best manager that I can possibly be. And if I need to go and watch Sutton, which is about 30 miles from here, but it takes three hours to get there on a Tuesday night, for the benefit of the players and for the benefit of the staff, then I'll do it. No one will outwork us.'

In March 2022 Wellens knew what he had to do to save Leyton Orient.

And he told the players straight away.

It was a meeting that changed everything.

'What are you going to bring to the group?'

First impressions count.

The day after the appointment of Richie Wellens, the club posted a video that gave everyone an insight into the character of their new manager.

'First of all, I'm buzzing to be here,' says Wellens, addressing the entire squad, who are sitting in front of him in the pavilion at the training ground. In his grey training top, he commands the floor and tells the players what they need to hear. It's what he truly believes, 'I think it's a really good club ... and there's some really talented footballers. But I do sense there's a little bit of tension. No one plays with a smile on their face. No one plays with freedom. So I've come to do my best to bring that back.'

He talks of taking the players on a journey with him, of being here in a year's time and 'popping it all over the place', but there's also an honest assessment of the recent performances. Showing character, yes, nicking points in the last minutes of games, yes, but not playing well. 'I just want one thing,' he says, first singling out Tom James, who he previously coached at Salford to kick things off, 'What are you going to bring to the group?'

Over the following few minutes each player lines up against a board at the front of the room, writing down the one thing they promise to do every day. Their non-negotiable contract with their new gaffer. Something they can control. Something they will commit to achieving daily. Once every player has pledged their commitment, Wellens reads over the board and addresses the team.

'Because you've given me one,' he says. 'I'll give you two. I'll give you honesty, I will always be honest with you. And

CHAPTER 16

I'll give you freedom. Whether it be at the training ground, or on the pitch. We'll have foundations to work from, but I'll give you freedom.'

And with that, Wellens asks the players if they're ready to train with a smile on their face, and the squad file outside.

The Richie Wellens era has begun.

'Like a scared dog'

It took place in another hotel.

Lawrence Vigouroux had been one of Leyton Orient's star players after signing on a free transfer in January 2020. Player of the year in the 2020/21 season, and well on his way to being awarded the same honour in 2022, he was, and is, a commanding goalkeeper, with great distribution, able to save points and keep the team in games like only the best goalkeepers can. He was vital to Orient's chances of getting out of the relegation battle they found themselves in.

But Vigouroux and Richie Wellens had history. And they needed to clear the air.

'I'm black and white, and I never play games with people,' says Wellens. 'If there's an issue, I get straight to the point.'

The 'issue' stemmed from their time together at Swindon, when Wellens was previously Vigouroux's manager. Expected back on the Tuesday from his time away with the Chilean national team, Vigouroux didn't walk back into training until the Friday morning. And with his first-choice goalkeeper absent without leave for most of the week, Wellens had to make a call. He promoted his backup stopper, Luke McCormick, to the starting 11 for his team's upcoming match.

Vigouroux didn't take the news well.

'I'm the manager of the football club,' explains Wellens. 'I've got to make a decision. If I allow him to dictate what

I do, then the other players will be watching me and going, "Hang on a minute."'

Wellens offered Vigouroux the chance to get his place back. '"Train well, you'll get back in. I love you to bits, just do this." He never did it,' says Wellens. 'So, I sacked him with about ten games to go.'

After an intervention from the Swindon chairman Lee Power, Wellens agreed to meet Vigouroux over the summer, to give him another chance to get back in the squad. All the goalkeeper needed to do was to prove his professionalism. To show his manager he had the right attitude.

'I met him in a cafe in Swindon,' says Wellens. 'We sat down on a really small table. We started talking. As I was talking to him, Lawrence's phone flashes up. He's got a WhatsApp message. But as I'm speaking to him, he picks his phone up, reads the message, and starts texting back. I pick my keys up. I pick my phone up, and I leave.'

The following season, Wellens won the League Two title with Swindon Town. Without the recently released Lawrence Vigouroux.

Wellens knew they would need to address their history. So did the hiring team.

'We maybe wouldn't have offered Richie the job if he wasn't going to be able to get on with Lawrence Vigouroux and Tom James,' says Matt Porter. 'That was massive for us. And that's bizarre, really. But we were like, "This is a red line. We have got to know." Because Tom was pretty much our best player at the time, along with Lawrence. "We've got to know that Richie can work with these two."'

Wellens invited Vigouroux to meet him at the Marriott Hotel, Waltham Abbey. After glowing recommendations from Martin Ling and Matt Harrold, Wellens was open to hearing what Vigouroux had to say. He was looking for an immediate reconciliation.

'He comes in like a scared dog,' remembers Wellens. 'And within five minutes, we laid it to rest. He went, "I've changed Gaffer, I promise you."'

That was all Wellens needed to hear.

He knows exactly what we need

The new boss's impact was instant.

After two well-managed draws away from home, including an impressive 1-1 draw at runaway league leaders Forest Green Rovers, Richie Wellens's newly invigorated Leyton Orient went on a three-game winning run, scoring eight goals and easing away from the relegation zone. With eight matches to go, Orient were suddenly 15 points clear of the drop, and virtually safe.

For club captain Darren Pratley, returning to action after being struck down with Covid, the change in the squad was immediately obvious.

'I remember thinking, "Oh, yeah, it feels like a proper club again,"' he tells me. 'The team was completely different from the team I left before Covid. The rotations, confidence, players demanding off each other. It was good.'

Pratley was well placed to comment. After the 2-0 victory over Barrow at the end of March, the veteran skipper had spoken to the club's official streaming service, Orient Live. He hadn't held back on just how bad things had got under the previous manager.

It was all in the detail.

'There were probably games in that period when we'd go out, and we probably wouldn't know what we were doing,' he told presenter Ollie Buck. 'We didn't know whether he [Kenny Jackett] was going to build from the back, [or he] was going to go long ... and there was big gaps between all the units. To the normal fan, if the gaps are massive ... and you can't quite get to that second ball, it looks like you're off the pace. [But now] having a manager who was a midfielder himself, he understands that if the gaps are too big, you can't get close to someone. He's given us a structure.'

Most damning perhaps were the words he spoke at the start of the interview, 'The [new] manager's not been retired too long himself. He understands what the boys want. The boys want to be coached. And long may that continue.'

Speaking to Pratley over a video call, he remembers the interview well.

'I gave a clear idea of what I felt we weren't doing and what needed to be changed,' he says. 'I think the connection between the fans and players had been lost. We had a little bit of uncertainty within the group, people getting left out, training with the kids. And sometimes when things are not going well, then it can affect you.'

After almost signing for Stevenage the previous summer, Pratley had a last-minute change of heart when Kenny Jackett phoned him and asked him to consider Leyton Orient. As a player under Jackett at Swansea, and immediately becoming his captain at the Os, Pratley is keen to clarify that the downturn in form shouldn't solely be laid at his former manager's door. But he's also adamant that the detail added to training and match preparation by Wellens was transformative.

'We'd gone from not too much detail in terms of what we want to do in possession, out of possession, set pieces, and all that sort of stuff. And then suddenly we'd work on it. So, we'd work through all different little patterns. We hadn't done that for most of the season. It was proper thorough.'

Having played against Wellens throughout his career ('Very good player. He could control the tempo of the game'), Pratley had been surprised when he first saw his former opponent in action as a manager.

'I played against his Swindon team for Charlton, and I remember him sitting in the stand just screaming at the

CHAPTER 16

players. I was thinking, "I don't remember him like that as a player."'

After picking up a further six points in the next four games after the Barrow victory, Orient travelled down the M4 to take on play-off chasing Swindon Town. Reduced to ten men after just 23 minutes, Orient fought hard to defeat Wellens's former club 2-1, both goals coming from Omar Beckles either side of half-time. It was a game that epitomised everything good about the team Wellens had started to build.

'We were up against it,' says Pratley. 'A couple of months before that, we would have probably gone under. We would probably have got beat four or five-nil. But it just galvanised us more to go and get the result.'

After the victory, Wellens allowed the club's media team into the changing room to film the post-match team talk. The clip, posted on YouTube, shows Aaron Drinan, a striker who hadn't stopped running all game, getting the plaudits from his manager.

'Aaron kept on taking us up the pitch,' explains Pratley. 'Driving with the ball 30, 40 yards, giving us a bit of a breather. And if it wasn't for him, we definitely wouldn't have got anything out of the game. It just showed us that if you work with the gaffer, you're going to get praise for doing the little stuff that people don't see.'

After just ten games, Wellens had transformed the team. His openness and willingness to invite the media team on to the training ground and into the changing room (along with some positive results) helped to rebuild a previously strained relationship with the supporters. He was also happy to address the fanbase directly, calling them out for negative chants, or unfair criticism. And at Swindon, for the first time, the large travelling support broke out into the Orient version of the song every fanbase was singing that year.

'We've got Super Richie Wellens. He knows exactly what we need. Beckles at the back. Drinan in attack. Orient going up the Football League.'

Things were once again looking up.

As Darren Pratley tells me, 'I had a feeling we'd have a good season the following season.'

17

Leyton Orient finish the 2021/22 season comfortably mid-table.

After using the last few games to assess his squad, Richie Wellens releases 11 players, including the campaign's second-highest goalscorer, Harry Smith.

Eight players come in. Fan favourite Theo Archibald signs a permanent contract and twinkle-toed midfielder George Moncur, son of former West Ham midfielder John Moncur, joins from Championship side Hull City.

They are soon joined by a loanee midfielder from Ipswich Town, 21-year-old Idris El Mizouni.

Club commentators and fan media can't help but compare the transformation under Richie Wellens to the way the club felt after Justin Edinburgh's first season.

The season before Edinburgh won the National League title.

'Sometimes alcohol can do that to you'

Like the change in fortunes towards the end of the campaign, the pre-season tour of Portugal also felt strangely similar to the events before Justin Edinburgh's title-winning year. Video diaries and behind-the-scenes clips filled YouTube and social media once again. They documented a group of players having fun, working hard and enjoying each other's company in the sun. A highly contested table tennis competition shows a group of players just as competitive in flip-flops and baseball caps as they are in football boots and shin pads.

For Darren Pratley, the staff and squad meal marked another turning point for the group.

'We [the staff and players] ended up in the same Irish bar,' he says. 'We were all singing and having a good time, laughing and joking, as you do when you're having a few drinks. And I think that brought the players and staff together. It was probably the main thing that made me think, "Oh, we've got something special here." Everyone was together. Everyone was happy. There were no cliques. Sometimes alcohol can do that to you.'

'We just built a special bond with the players and the staff,' adds Dan Happe. 'It was all as one.'

Bond formed, buzz building, all that remained was to get some pre-season friendlies into the team's legs. But even before the season started, injuries were mounting up, particularly in attacking areas. As a result, Richie Wellens had to change his approach. He had to build from the back.

'I was always a manager that loved attacking, loved thinking about how we're going to play against the opposition. But that helped me. It changed my thinking,' he tells me.

Despite a very mixed series of pre-season results, the coaching staff were optimistic about the season to come.

'Can we get to the play-offs?' says Paul Terry. 'That was our first aim.'

Terry talks about 'a little dungeon of a room' during the pre-season tour in Portugal where Wellens mapped out what the season was going to look like for the group. The graph went upwards, but it didn't go in a straight line.

CHAPTER 17

'It's going to have a real messy part in the middle of the season and then we'll get to where we want to get to,' Wellens told the group.

For everyone involved, belief was there from the outset.

What nobody could foresee was how the season would start.

George Moncur, my Lord
Saturday, 30 July 2022, Brisbane Road
Leyton Orient 2 Grimsby Town 0

Leyton Orient haven't scored a penalty for 100 consecutive league games. Three minutes into the second half of their opening match of the season, George Moncur breaks the curse from the penalty spot; 1-0 up, Orient are on their way.

Moncur is on his debut, but he doesn't shy away from his responsibilities when the opportunity arises. Despite missing a penalty in pre-season, he has a belief that a higher power is there to help.

'I bring Jesus into it because I believe he breaks chains,' he says, a few weeks later in an interview with the *Evening Standard*. 'He breaks curses and there was definitely a curse around that penalty spot at Orient. For me to step up and score, I give God all the glory for that, because I believe he broke a curse there.'

The upcoming winter World Cup in Qatar means the EFL season is starting in July, the first time it has got going so early since the end of the second world war. For the crowd, it is odd to be watching a competitive league match so early in the year. The sun is behind the clouds, but it is hot and bright. Everyone in shorts and sunglasses. It is very much pre-season weather.

However, despite the heat, and it still being July, it doesn't feel like a pre-season match. Grimsby Town, recently promoted from the National League, were always going to be a tricky prospect. After defeating Solihull Moors, Notts County and Wrexham in the previous season's play-offs, the Mariners are out to prove they are a big club, back in the Football League where they belong. The away end is packed and bouncing, full of black and white and optimism. A big day out in the capital. On the beers in the sun.

Grimsby start well, living up to expectations. But after Moncur's converted penalty, Lawrence Vigouroux is never really threatened in the Orient goal.

Seven minutes after the penalty, it is over. And in spectacular fashion. A floated corner from Theo Archibald is partially cleared by the Grimsby defence, landing just outside the box, where Orient full-back Tom James is lurking. Back from last season's extended injury absence, James wastes no time in making his mark back in the team. The ball bounces once, sitting up perfectly for James to strike with his left foot. From nearly 30 yards out his shot flies into the top corner. One of the most perfect strikes you could ever hope to see. He couldn't have hit it any sweeter.

'What a goal, what a goal from Tom James,' screams Dave Victor on commentary. 'That was special.'

It truly is. Striker Ruel Sotiriou, entering his sixth season at the club he joined through the youth team, stands with his hands on his head, almost in disbelief at what he's just seen.

The whole team celebrate with James. It's just what they needed. A buffer towards a routine three points. Starting the season off with a win. A clean sheet, a spectacular goal and surprisingly little drama. It is a sign of things to come.

'Boy, this is it'

Leyton Orient don't lose any of their first ten matches.

In fact, the team won nine out of those first ten. After an impressive 2-0 away victory at Barrow at the end of

CHAPTER 17

September, Orient sit top of League Two, undefeated on 28 points. It is an exceptional start to the season.

'We were like, "Boy, this is it,"' remembers Dan Happe. '"This could be the one, here." We were keeping clean sheets for fun. It seemed easy to us.'

Defeating Barrow at Holker Street, who up until that match hadn't lost all season at home, was no easy task. 'They were flying at the start,' adds Happe. 'We were going there thinking, "This could be a tough game." And then we absolutely schooled them 2-0.'

Richie Wellens recalls talking to Kent Teague and fellow American board member Nick Semaca after the first ten games. They were already feeling confident. Wellens remembers what they told him, 'If you fuck this up, man ... we're going to look like fools.'

Wellens didn't disagree. But for him, the belief started well before the match at Barrow. Away at Swindon on a Tuesday night for the fourth fixture of the season, Orient left with a draw in a game they probably should have won.

'It was the only time we dropped points,' says Wellens. And it was like, "We're a good team." I think that was the moment where the players thought, "You know what? We can actually do this."'

I ask him if he thought he was going to get the team promoted by the end of the season, even at such an early stage of the campaign.

'Yeah,' he replies, without hesitation. 'After those ten games, you get 28 points. You then only need 50 points from 36 [matches]. And I'll go back to Kent and Nick's phrase, "If you fuck this up, we're going to look like fools." And that's the way that I felt.'

Ten games, nine wins, seven clean sheets.

There was something very exciting happening down at Brisbane Road.

The X Factor

For captain Darren Pratley, the difference between Orient and the rest of the league in those first few months was simple. 'I think we had better players,' he says. 'We had a team working hard for each other. We had a team knowing what they were going to do. And then we had a little bit of X Factor in Smithy.'

Paul Smyth, the diminutive Northern Irish international, was already providing some magic that season. Signed from Championship team QPR by Kenny Jackett, he spent much of his first campaign under Jackett out of the team with injuries. A rapid winger, with four goals in those first ten games, he was now tearing defences apart at will, scoring spectacular goals for fun under Richie Wellens.

While Orient's little bit of X Factor was making the game look easy, everyone else was gelling together perfectly as well. Lawrence Vigouroux in goal was already proving why he would be on the books of a Premier League team within the year. Dan Happe, Adam Thompson and new PFA chair Omar Beckles were keeping clean sheets in the centre of defence, backed up by Jayden Sweeney, Rob Hunt and Tom James, the latter matching Smyth for spectacular goals from full-back. Idris El Mizouni was living in a different age, breathing life into the role of a box-to-box midfielder. Jordan Brown and Darren Pratley were controlling the middle of the pitch, backed up by Craig Clay playing his sixth season with the club. Theo Archibald, Ruel Sotiriou and George Moncur were skipping past defences, racking up goals and chipping in with assists alongside Smyth. Aaron Drinan and on-loan striker Charlie Kelman were putting in a shift every game, working hard to close down the opposition as the manager had instructed. It was a team that built from the back. A team that defended from the front. They had a plan. It was working.

CHAPTER 17

And there was something special going on in the dressing room. A feeling, a vibe, the perfect combination of players, coaches and, of course, manager.

'He delegates really well,' says Paul Terry, when I ask him about working with Richie Wellens. 'He gives you an opinion. He'll ask your opinion. He's very detailed in what he wants. He knows how he wants his teams to play. And he's very good at seeing things. He can watch a team, and in seconds, he knows exactly how he wants to play against them.'

The clarity from the manager, and his openness and communication was reflected among the staff and the way they managed the squad.

'We give them their own space,' says Terry. 'I keep it relaxed with the players. But when we go out to warm up, we're ready for a game. They know that when it's time to work, it's time to *work*. And a lot of work goes into the characters we bring into the dressing room.'

Pratley recalls seeing George Moncur for the first time and how very quickly, despite his cocksure persona, the new signing integrated into the group.

'I remember his interview when he came in,' says Pratley. 'I was thinking, "Who's this kid with the Gucci shirt? What have we signed here?"' Alongside the lairy shirts, it was soon very clear that Moncur's religious beliefs were also a distinctive part of his personality. 'He was quite open,' continues Pratley. 'And normally the group might take the mickey out of you if you're a little bit different. But the group really bought in to what he was bringing to the team.'

While Moncur was inviting the squad to join him in prayer if they were interested ('At one point, there was 20 lads in there. Just going in to have a look and listening to what they're saying'), Pratley is keen to highlight the importance of another big personality.

'Then you've got other characters like Theo [Archibald]. Theo loves London. He lives in Hackney. Dresses a bit strange. And everyone takes to him because he probably gets taken the mick out of with the clothes he wears. He wears clothes at least 15 sizes too big for him. He rides his bike to the game. He does some crazy stuff, the boy. But he's another character, a big character in the changing room. I think everyone's accepted no matter what you are, what you believe in. Leyton as a place is a bit like that as well, isn't it? It's diverse. Everyone's welcome.'

And it doesn't hurt when you're winning every week.

But of course, that couldn't last.

Not a crisis
Monday, 2 January 2023, Sixfields Stadium

Northampton Town 1 Leyton Orient 0

The Orient Outlook Podcast called it a 'mini-crisis'. Just like in 2018/19, it started after Christmas.

The team had only lost twice since July, an achievement that left Leyton Orient top of League Two by the end of 2022. After 0-0 draws with Newport County and title rivals Stevenage, Richie Wellens's team were five points clear of second-placed Stevenage on New Year's Day.

Promotion back to League One, as well as the League Two title, were now both Orient's to lose.

Northampton Town sat in third place, ten points behind Orient. When the Os visited their Sixfields Stadium on 2 January, it felt like a big game.

It was not Orient's day.

After just 18 minutes, things start to go wrong. Dan Happe, having his best season so far for the club, is taken off injured. Part of the central defensive partnership alongside Omar Beckles, he has helped to keep an incredible 15 clean

CHAPTER 17

sheets from the 23 league matches played since the start of the season.

'I was probably playing the best football I had for a long time,' says Happe. 'And then I go and get injured at a pinnacle moment, after Christmas. That's when the good games start coming. That's when the games that matter really start coming. And then we had a little bit of a crumble.'

Orient have their chances against Northampton, but the game is still goalless at half-time. Just five minutes into the second half, Orient are 1-0 down. Things get worse when Beckles has a goal disallowed for a marginal offside decision. Finally, Orient's misery is compounded when replacement centre back Shad Ogie hobbles off injured and Beckles's frustration spills over, seeing him sent off for elbowing his opponent in stoppage time.

After having the best defence in the entire division, Orient are suddenly without three of their first-choice centre-backs: Beckles suspended for three games, Happe and Ogie ruled out with injury for the foreseeable future.

For the next two games, Orient attempt to steady the ship. A stunning volley from Theo Archibald from well outside the box secures three points at home to Doncaster. This is followed by a frustrating 0-0 draw at home to Barrow. The match sees another defensive setback when Tom James is sent off for two bookable offences deep into injury time.

What Orient didn't need was a trip to face second-placed Stevenage and their boss Steve Evans, the man who managed Rotherham in 2014, defeating the Os at Wembley in that painful play-off final. With emergency cover being drafted in for the defence in the form of loanees Ed Turns and Jamie McCart, it was always going to be tough for Orient to get something from the game. It wasn't helped by the fact that they were 2-0 down after 11 minutes, and down to ten men by half-time, Idris El Mizouni shown a red card for yet two more bookable offences.

The game ends 3-0 and Orient lose their next one as well, 1-0 away at Tranmere, with Beckles returning from suspension and scoring an unfortunate own goal in the 82nd minute.

The phrase 'mini-crisis' flew around social media and the seriousness of the loss of form was debated across the fanbase. Despite Orient still being top of the league by two points, Stevenage and Northampton both had games in hand. Os supporters remembered the 2013/14 season, when form dropped off and the team played themselves out of the automatic promotion spots and into the play-offs, before the pain of defeat in the final.

For Dan Happe, battling back from injury and unable to help, it was tough to watch.

'I started thinking we could bottle this here,' he says. 'I was pooing my pants, let's be honest.'

And another tough local derby was up next.

Wimbledon at home on the following Saturday was suddenly a must-win game.

He's behind you
Saturday, 4 February 2023, Brisbane Road
Leyton Orient 1 AFC Wimbledon 0

Brisbane Road is full of big-game energy. Another packed away end and a proper London derby. Orient need a win. Orient want revenge.

The reverse fixture at Plough Lane back in November had seen Wimbledon win 2-0, the second goal coming from pantomime villain Harry Pell. A tall, aggressive midfielder, Pell is the sort of player that knows how to wind-up opposition fans and players, often just by walking on to the pitch. His

CHAPTER 17

goal, plus Jordan Brown's disallowed 'start of a comeback' strike, had added salt into Orient's wounds. There was also some heavy-handed stewarding in the away end. Punches were thrown and the police steamed in. Orient felt wronged both on and off the pitch. It was a night to forget.

Back at Brisbane Road, everything goes to plan. Wimbledon miss some clear chances in the second half, before George Moncur skips past the opposition defence, his twinkle toes twinkling just perfectly before striking a shot low and hard into the bottom corner. It is one of those collective, guttural releases of relief and joy from the home crowd. Soon afterwards, Pell is substituted to the sound of appropriate pantomime jeers. From that point on, Orient never look like losing.

As much as many fans, and the injured Dan Happe may have been worried after those defeats in January, most of the players and staff were confident it was just a small blip. After all, Richie Wellens had predicted it would come at some point during the season. In Richie we trust was the clear message from most of the club's more level-headed followers.

Owner Nigel Travis, sitting upstairs in the gallery at Brisbane Road or at his home in Boston, wasn't worried.

'I felt very confident from October on,' he says. 'And I never really didn't feel confident after that. One of the reasons was we kept scoring these wonder goals. We had all the worldies from Paul Smyth, and I remember having a conversation with Richie and Martin, "Why the hell can't we score some scrambled goals?!"'

Smyth's 'worldie' overhead kick away at Doncaster back in October would go on to win the goal of the season award, but Theo Archibald and Tom James were seemingly able to score from every part of the pitch as well. It just added to the confidence running through the squad. For captain Darren

Pratley, he knew his team had the quality to turn January's results around.

'There was never a point when you'd come into the changing room where you'd think, "Oh, they're struggling with confidence," even when we had that bad run. We still believed we could do it.

'It's crazy because when you're winning every week, you just don't feel like you're going to lose,' he adds. 'You feel like every pass is simple. Everything you do, every phase, it's just happening. You're not really thinking about things. If we lost the game, we'd be like, "All right, next week. We'll win the next one."'

The next one, the 1-0 victory over Wimbledon, also holds significance because it marks the first clean sheet for the new central defensive partnership of Omar Beckles and emergency loan signing Ed Turns. Turns, who came from Premier League club Brighton & Hove Albion, was only 20 years old, and after a slightly shaky start, soon settled into the team.

The mini-crisis officially over, the Os could focus on building momentum and targeting enough points to secure automatic promotion.

They didn't lose another game until mid-April.

'Like a dog with two dicks'
Friday, 7 April 2023, the Peninsula Stadium
Salford City 0 Leyton Orient 2

Everyone has their favourite game that season. The one that felt most important. The one that seemed to matter most.

For Dan Happe it was the one immediately before the Salford clash, Carlisle at home. Down to ten men, Orient somehow held on to a 1-0 lead against a team also chasing promotion. The win left Orient seven points clear of second-

CHAPTER 17

placed Northampton, going into the Easter weekend ten games unbeaten.

Richie Wellens's return to Salford City couldn't have gone much better. On a glorious day in April, Orient's heaving away support packs out the away end, shielding their eyes from the warm spring sun as they watch their team tear apart the opposition.

It is one of the most complete performances of the season, a first half where everything comes together, when Orient truly look like the team seven points clear at the top of the league. It is the sort of performance supporters haven't seen too many times. Orient's results over the course of the season have been steady, impressive, gathering points and keeping clean sheets without too much drama. Consistent and competent. Tight and in control.

Against Salford, they blow their opponents away.

'Different class ... men against boys first half,' says Wellens, describing his team's performance to Dave Victor in the post-match interview. 'And the celebrations at the end were pretty special as well.'

Wellens leads his team in the passionate celebrations with the away support at the end of the match. He has every reason to feel jubilant. The 2-0 win has seen a lovely finish from Ruel Sotiriou open the scoring, before a complete team goal, full of crisp passing from defence to attack is finished off by George Moncur, who celebrates by getting his belly out and slapping it in front of the home fans. It isn't the only time Orient fans see the midfielder's belly that season.

For Wellens, the result, and performance is that much sweeter because it was against his old club. I asked him how he felt after the win.

'How do you think it felt?' he says, with a smile. 'I was like a dog with two dicks.'

A few weeks earlier on Sky Sports, Gary Neville and Jamie Carragher had discussed the imminent sacking of Antonio Conte by Spurs. Neville had suggested that Tottenham should stick with their manager, despite Conte's criticism of some aspects of the club. In the social media exchange that followed, Carragher pointed to Neville's sacking of Richie Wellens as an example of his colleague's hypocrisy.

'Why didn't you do that with Richie Wellens after he criticised Salford & the players in public!!' said Carragher.

'Conte is in 4th place. We were in free fall, 6-points off play-offs in 9th, with the largest budget in the league,' replied Neville. 'I do know. I was watching.'

Addressing the tweet at the time, Wellens is defiant.

'Look, he's made a judgement that I wasn't good enough to manage this club, so ... we move on,' he tells Dave Victor. 'I don't think I was given the best shot ... everybody else here was given £3m, £4m. I was given 50p and a bag of crisps.'

Looking back, Wellens can see that his time at Salford, although disappointing, ultimately made him a better manager.

'It was a big learning curve for me because at that stage of my career, I wasn't managing upwards very well at all. I've learned a lot from that, because I've got a lot of respect for Gary. But I didn't show it a lot of the time.'

The win meant Orient were still top of the league, and now 11 points ahead of fourth spot, with the top three teams promoted automatically.

'That was another step,' Wellens tells me. 'That felt like another big win. That was the one that I thought, yeah, we're definitely promoted.'

With just seven games to go, even the most pessimistic Orient fan was struggling to disagree.

CHAPTER 17

Typical Orient
Tuesday, 18 April 2023, Priestfield Stadium
Gillingham 2 Leyton Orient 0

In April 2023, Orient supporters experienced one of the greatest, most unique nights you could hope to be a part of as a football fan.

It has been just 14 months since one of the worst. The night I fell over and ripped my jeans, tore open my knee and then watched on, juggling both physical and emotional pain as Leyton Orient were ripped apart by Bristol Rovers on a horrible Tuesday night at Brisbane Road. The night Kenny Jackett was sacked.

On Tuesday, 18 April 2023, Richie Wellens's team travelled to Kent to take on a Gillingham side who were still fighting to secure their EFL status for another season. In contrast, Orient knew that a win would secure promotion back into League One. And with Gillingham only a short train ride away from east London, the away allocation had been sold out for weeks. Everyone knew this could be the game. Nobody wanted to miss it.

Just three days earlier, Orient won 2-0 away at Sutton United. Kieran Sadlier had opened the scoring with a direct free kick, before Tom James scored another stunner from outside the box. It was a strike so sweet that it caused Ruel Sotiriou to replicate his celebration from James's goal during the opening game of the season, running with his hands on his head, his mouth wide open in shock.

There was also shock at the end of the match. Sky Sports announced that the win had secured Orient's promotion. It hadn't; they needed one more game.

I manage to squeeze on to a commuter train out of Stratford, juggling a Dutch-courage beer alongside other people's laptops and judging looks. It is a relief to hear the sound of other cans cracking open as we roll out of east London towards Gillingham. The train is full of Orient, we just can't see each other. We soon would.

As you walk up from the station, you see the away end in the distance. Priestfield is one of those old grounds in the middle of terraced houses, one of those walks to a ground that drips in nostalgia. Orient fans queueing up to get in, working their way up the bank of makeshift seating that rises on temporary scaffolding behind the goal, it soon dispels the nostalgia dream. As you walk on to the steps it makes a noise, it starts to rattle. 'Anything could happen, tonight,' you think.

After just 14 minutes, it did.

Orient are all over the home team.

Sharp, incisive, flowing football – moving the ball like a team destined for promotion. 'We looked like a proper, proper team,' remembers Dan Happe.

They are a team that know they are better than everyone else. A team completely in control. And then Omar Beckles makes a last-ditch tackle, doesn't get enough of the ball and is shown a red card by referee Carl Brook. Orient are suddenly down to ten men. 'We were just popping it about and then we got a red card and the game changed,' says Happe. To make things even worse, Gillingham score from the resulting free kick.

Typical Orient.

The lads push for an equaliser, but it isn't happening and in the 76th minute, Idris El Mizouni handles the ball in the penalty box. Cheye Alexander converts the resulting penalty, Gillingham are 2-0 up and it is game over. With Bradford drawing at Swindon, and Northampton winning away at Sutton, Orient are going to have to wait for promotion. Not tonight, Os. Not tonight.

Things then take a turn for the farcical. With 78 minutes on the clock, the lights simply go out. A proper 'Who forgot

CHAPTER 17

to put some money in the meter?' 1970s floodlight failure. The playing surface and the stands are plunged into darkness and the teams leave the field. It is a bit of a mess.

Typical bloody Orient.

And then.

As we stand there, on our rickety scaffold, wondering if we're going to see any more football, the stadium illuminated by lights from people's phones, we get some news. It's piecemeal, hardly anyone has a decent service on their mobiles, but enough people have seen the score for it to be legit.

Swindon have scored against Bradford. If the scores stay the same, Orient will be promoted. The away end erupts.

It's a surreal experience. The lights eventually come back on, and the players lethargically take the field. Within minutes, there's more news. The final whistle has blown at the County Ground. Swindon, the team Orient played when that first relegation under Francesco Becchetti was confirmed almost eight years earlier, have beaten Bradford.

It's official. Orient will be promoted. The Os are back in League One.

'Leyton Orient are celebrating on the pitch even though their game hasn't finished,' says the BBC, covering that night's EFL matches on their website. 'What a strange way to go up. Not that they'll care!'

Dan Happe, on his way back from injury certainly doesn't.

'All the staff, all the players on the bench, we're literally running on the pitch,' he recalls. 'We huddled around in the middle, just jumping around. All the fans are just watching us jump ... It's a bit disrespectful, to be honest. But at the time, emotions just took over, didn't they? It was mad. It was completely crazy. It was honestly a moment I'll remember for the rest of my life.'

For Martin Ling, sitting in the directors' box, it is the best moment of the season.

'Being in the box, it was always talked about [the staff] looking up to see me because I'll have the correct scores. But things are all over the place. And I remember the eye contact of Richie and me and the players, because they don't want to run on to the pitch until we actually get it confirmed.'

At this point, Ling pauses.

'The hairs on the back of my neck are standing up now!' he says, remembering the moment the score was verified on his feed upstairs. 'The explosion of me giving two thumbs up and saying "let them go mad" and that scene of them all running on the pitch ... I've never been at a match like it.'

'It was brilliant,' remembers Matt Simpson, who was in the stand behind the goal. 'But it was definitely confirmed in the least sort of exciting, least glamorous way possible – just waiting to see if another team had dropped points when we were losing anyway. A totally Orient way to do it.'

Eventually, the referee regains control of the match, and the last few minutes are played out in a celebratory procession. Orient promoted whatever happens, Gillingham happy that their victory has secured their League Two status, the two teams barely break into a jog.

It is well past 10pm when the final whistle eventually blows. Keren Harrison is clock-watching. '"Why the hell did I come by train?" she remembers thinking. '"I've now got to try and get home. I can't stay for the end of all the celebrations!"'

And the celebrations are big. First a pitch invasion, at least a third of the travelling fans running on to the grass. They are soon hemmed into the penalty area by the security staff using a long rope as a makeshift barrier. The Orient players are on the other side shaking hands and hugging fans – joy on everyone's faces.

CHAPTER 17

Eventually, the pitch is cleared, and the official EFL-sanctioned promotion celebrations can begin. Champagne and bottles of beer for the players and staff, they dance around with 'Sky Bet League Two' flags bearing the words 'Promoted' and 'We stepped up' as photographers get their pictures and Sky Sports attempt an interview with Richie Wellens.

In the stands we look on as Kent Teague makes his way on to the pitch to join in the fun. Kent in Kent.

'I remember asking Richie, "Can I step on to the pitch now?"' he tells me. 'And he was like, "Mate, you could have stepped on the pitch anytime you please, but yes, I'll give you my approval."'

As the players and staff celebrate in front of the fans, another key member of the team is thrust into the limelight by the players. Ada Martin, kit manager and club ever-present, is roundly applauded by both the staff and supporters, giving fistbumps towards the stands to a chorus of passionate cheers.

I ask Ada if that year's squad made him feel a part of things in a particularly special way.

'It's more me making them part of the team than the other way!' he says. 'I can speak from experience. I was there going down to the National League with a team full of kids completely gone on their arses. It's integrating them into my way of thinking, "You know about the Italians, but I don't think you *really* know. This is massive today, because we were in League One when they took us over, and now we're back in League One. So, you're part of history. I don't think you realise it, but you're massively part of the history of the club."'

Ada explains how he had encouraged the team to go and watch the Dream Team *Love of the Game* series, the show that documented Orient down in the National League.

'Justin was in it. I was in it. Just look at it. Go on, have a look. And it will show you what this club was like,' he told them.

Many of the players took Ada's advice.

'When people know you've been there for such a long time, the players catch,' he continues. 'They know what it means to you, more as a fan than as someone who works for the club. It's like, "We're doing this for you." That's what it felt like that night. It was a crazy night. We were still in the ground at about a quarter to midnight when there are stewards wanting to go home.'

The following day, the club released a video showing the team still celebrating on the coach as they drive home, one of the players streaming 'Pump It Up!', a remix of the club classic by DJ Endor. As the players and staff sing, 'Don't you know pump it up, the Os are going up!' with their beers in hand, everyone is left wondering, can the team go one better?

Will Leyton Orient win the league as well?

A sea of red
Saturday, 22 April 2023, Brisbane Road
Leyton Orient 2 Crewe Alexandra 0

Four days later, they did.

In a press release earlier in the week, Richie Wellens put a call out for supporters to bring their scarves to the final home matches of the season.

'I have seen other sets of supporters, whether that be club or international, have a stadium full of supporters holding their scarves up high,' he said on the club's website. 'And it can make the hairs stand up on the back of your neck. That's why the players, and the staff and myself WANT you to bring your scarves, make as much noise as you can, and show just how proud we are to be Leyton Orient Football Club.'

As the surprising dressing room anthem 'Wagon Wheel' (more on this later) fades out over the PA system and the

CHAPTER 17

referee prepares to blow his whistle for kick-off, Wellens looks around the stadium. His plea has been answered. Brisbane Road is a 'sea of red', scarves held high, supporters young and old, swinging them around their heads in celebration. A roar of anticipation greets the kick-off, because this is it. Leyton Orient, a team on the edge of liquidation, plummeting out of existence six years earlier, are now on the brink of a second league title in the space of just four years.

The task ahead of Wellens and his team becomes easier 11 minutes into the match when Stevenage, the only team also able to claim the championship, go a goal down against play-off chasing Mansfield Town. When George Moncur wraps up the season the way he had started it, converting a penalty in front of the South Stand to put Orient 1-0 up, the first strains of 'Campeones' begin to ring out from the stands.

In the 77th minute, striker Charlie Kelman pounces on a defensive mistake, rounds the keeper and runs the ball into an empty net. The title is inevitable. The rest of the match a procession, and as the game finishes, with Orient winning 2-0, the fans invade the pitch in celebration. Once again, Leyton Orient are champions.

It is an extraordinary achievement.

I ask Wellens what he remembers of that day.

'Just a blur,' he says. 'I remember Mark Devlin walking past me with a red scarf and I took his red scarf, and I started waving it around my head, and then everyone followed. And that was a brilliant memory. I remember Moncur scoring a penalty. I remember the goalkeeper coming out and missing it and thinking, "Right, Kelman can't miss this." That's probably the only three things that I remember about that game.'

As the fans crowd around the players, held back by a makeshift security cordon near the dugouts, a microphone is passed around. There's spontaneous karaoke from the squad, leading the supporters in a chorus of terrace chants down on the Brisbane Road turf.

For Wellens, celebrating with his team, it is the ultimate justification for taking the job in the first place. And for doing things his way.

'I have full power in terms of picking the tactics, picking the players. No one is over my shoulder. I have a very clear vision of the way that I want to play. And when people cloud that vision, I just don't like it. I don't interfere with the finances of the club. I'm not going to tell Nigel how to run a football club or Lingy how to do his job, because they're better at their job than me. And I think it's important when you go into a football club, you can create an environment where people enjoy working, and more than anything, you empower them to do their own job. And I think that's what I'm good at.'

I ask him the same question I'd asked Martin Ling: he came in to save Leyton Orient, but did Leyton Orient also save him?

'Yeah, 100 per cent,' he replies, without hesitation. 'I would only ever pick a club that is suited to the way that I want to play, with character. And what I'm most proud of with this Leyton Orient team – they reflect me. They reflect me as a person.

'They reflect the way that I want my teams to play, with high energy, with hunger. And I think that reflects well on the people. When they come and watch their team, they can be proud of what they're seeing.'

One week later, Wellens's team lifted the championship trophy in front of another packed Brisbane Road crowd. His team had lost to promotion-chasing Stockport County, but it didn't matter. Nigel Travis placed the trophy on the plinth before Darren Pratley along with Omar Beckles and Ada

CHAPTER 17

Martin lifted it to a backdrop of fireworks and jets of red and white smoke.

Like Justin Edinburgh before him, Richie Wellens had made every Leyton Orient supporter proud once again. And this time, the celebrations lasted for weeks.

18

'Everyone was just in the best mood ever. I can't put into words how good it was. Just coming to training with a smile on your face, every day. I was waking up, getting out of bed, skipping to the shower. Honestly. It was brilliant.'

Dan Happe, on winning his second league title with Leyton Orient

Wagon Wheels

Darius Rucker is the Grammy award-winning lead singer of Hootie & the Blowfish as well as a massively successful solo artist. A member of the Country Music Association Hall of Fame and the first black American to win the New Artist Award from the CMA, he has over 1.5 million followers on X and nearly one million on Instagram.

In April 2023, he replied to a tweet from Leyton Orient.

A couple of weeks earlier, after promotion was secured at Gillingham, the club posted a video from the celebrations in the dressing room at Priestfield. It showed the players and staff, beers in hand, jumping around, passionately singing along to a song that most Orient fans had never heard before. Lyrics talked of the 'land of the pines', North Carolina and praying to God. The rousing chorus, 'Rock me mama like a wagon wheel ... rock me mama any way you feel', was belted out with passion to a man by everyone in the room.

The song was 'Wagon Wheel', Rucker's multimillion-selling cover of a track originally co-written by Bob Dylan.

CHAPTER 18

Released in 2013, Rucker's version reached number 15 in the US Billboard Hot 100.

'This is awesome,' replied the singer to the video, before following up with a quote tweet to his millions of followers, 'This is my new favorite Soccer team. Congratulations boys... Just like The Jeffersons. We are moving on up!!!!'

The reference to *The Jeffersons*, a CBS sitcom that ran in the 1970s and 80s in the US but was never broadcast in the UK, further emphasises the different worlds Leyton Orient and country music superstar Darius Rucker inhabit. Just why had the team adopted a country music cover of 'Wagon Wheel' as their anthem?

'That bloody "Wagon Wheel" song came out of nowhere,' says Paul Terry, recalling sitting in the staff room at Brisbane Road earlier in the season and hearing music coming from the changing room. 'I remember the gaffer going, "What's this song they keep playing? I ain't got a clue what it is, but they play it all the time."'

Inevitably, George Moncur was responsible.

'He's got this playlist where he has all sorts of songs,' explains Dan Happe. 'He's very religious, so he'll bring these religious songs in, and everyone just jumps on it and everyone starts to sing. And one of them was "Wagon Wheel". If we won, it would be the very first song that we played. It was a little party song for us. I started listening to it in my car and all sorts.'

Barry Galvin is Orient's matchday announcer. Like so many people involved with the club, he's a lifelong supporter. A decade earlier, his son became 'the face of Orient despair' when the Sky Sports cameras cut to his anguished face after Alex Revel scored his worldie of an equaliser for Rotherham at Wembley.

Ten years later, Barry became one of the many faces of Orient joy.

After seeing the 'Wagon Wheel' celebration video, Barry got in touch with Luke Lambourne, the club's press officer. He had a proposal for the Crewe match.

I said, "Look, I can bring my guitar, go down to the changing room, and we'll have a singsong afterwards." And Luke went, "What's it going to be like?" I said, "Well, Luke, thanks for your confidence."

Lambourne needn't have worried. Fifteen minutes after the end of the match, Barry enters the changing room with his guitar. The party is already well under way.

'I said, "Guys, Darius Rucker can't make it. Substitution." And I started playing it, and they all immediately joined in.'

It is a joyous moment, captured in the club's celebration video. Barry leads the team as they jump and sing in front of him. Young defender Jayden Sweeney appears at the door late, wondering what the hell is going on. Ruel Sotiriou leads the squad in spraying beer all over Barry's head. By the time Barry's rendition finishes, and they break into a chorus of 'We are going up, say are we going up,' his black shirt is drenched to the skin.

'I was very happy,' says Barry. 'Who wouldn't want to be in the dressing room, celebrating with the players? Honestly, that was one of the best days of my life.'

19

In the final game of the 2022/23 season, Orient draw 1–1 away at Bradford City in front of over 22,000 supporters. Richie Wellens's team finish the season on 91 points, six clear of second-place Stevenage.

The owners pay for the players and staff to go on a holiday to Marbella to celebrate the club's return to League One. When asked if he could share any anecdotes from that trip, captain Darren Pratley replies, with a smile, 'Probably not, no.'

There are two high-profile departures over the summer. Top scorer and goal of the season winner Paul Smyth re-signs for Championship club QPR. Goalkeeper and player of the season Lawrence Vigouroux signs for Vincent Kompany's Burnley after their promotion to the Premier League.

Leyton Orient are scheduled to play their first game of the new season back in England's third tier away at local rivals Charlton Athletic.

A small flirt
Saturday, 5 August 2023, The Valley
Charlton Athletic 1 Leyton Orient 0

It felt different.

Just six years earlier, Leyton Orient were playing at Guiseley in front of 4,000 fans in the National League. Now, they were playing Charlton Athletic at The Valley in front of 18,500. Over 3,000 Orient supporters packed out the away end behind the goal, the giant stands of The Valley looming over us, rising high into the humid summer sky. Orient were back. And the 1-0 defeat showed promise. The team could hold their own at this level.

After a tough start, Richie Wellens's young team began to find form. On Phoenix FM's *The Orient Hour* we discussed being satisfied with a mid-table finish by the end of the season. A small flirt with the play-offs would be a bonus.

And that's exactly what happened. There were some real highs (the last-minute winner from Ruel Sotiriou in a 4-3 victory over Northampton; the 3-0 away defeat of eventual league winners Portsmouth; the emergence of an atmosphere creating drum in the North and South stands) but, due to an unfortunate series of injuries, there were the inevitable lows as well.

Still, by March, after a satisfying 1-0 away win at Stevenage, Orient sat just five points off the play-offs. However, two defeats over Easter saw the play-off dream die. In April, Orient lost 3-0 away to Derby in front of over 30,000 fans. It was men against boys.

'They ran all over us,' said Richie Wellens, after the match. 'The players have been unbelievable this year, but they're probably just on their last legs and we're asking too much of them with what we've got available ... we just ran out of steam a little bit.'

As the Orient express chugged towards the end of the season, finishing in a respectable 11th place on 65 points, Orient fans began to look to the future.

Solidly mid-table. Back in League One. Back where this story started. Something to build on.

CHAPTER 19

'I told him he was absolutely bonkers'

Craig Clay played an instrumental part in getting Orient back into League One. Although he was part of the group of players released in the summer of 2023, the midfielder holds the honour alongside Dan Happe, Sam Sergeant and Matt Harrold (in Harrold's case as a player, then a coach) of winning both the National League and League Two with Leyton Orient.

His words, summed up by the Orient press team after the achievement in 2023, perfectly encapsulate how people associated with Orient felt.

'Justin started this, and Richie's finished it.'

Speaking to Justin Edinburgh's son, Charlie, I ask him if he remembers how he felt when his dad took on the Orient job.

'I told him he was absolutely bonkers,' says Charlie. 'But he backed himself. And I see a lot of similarity with Richie. Dad was never prepared to settle for that one league title. I know how much he was relishing getting into League Two. And in his mind, he would have thought that they could have gone up automatically again.'

Charlie now runs the JE3 Foundation – an organisation set up in his father's honour, that educates and trains staff and volunteers on how to react to sudden cardiac arrest, while providing defibrillators to sports venues. They are also campaigning for Justin's Law, which would involve changing the law to ensure all UK health and sports facilities are equipped with a defibrillator.

For Charlie, fundraising and talking about his dad every day is a comfort. 'It's almost like he's still here with me,' he says. 'It was my coping mechanism with grief. It got me out of bed every morning. It kept my brain occupied.'

In January 2020, Leyton Orient re-named the main West Stand after Justin. I ask Charlie what that day was like.

'There were tears,' he says. 'It was overwhelming. I don't really have the words, to be honest.'

Still, there was laughter among the tears. Charlie explains how Justin would have loved to have had a stand named after him. 'He wouldn't have stopped going on about it, "I've got a stand named after me!"'

Charlie looks like his dad. He sounds like his dad as well. His work at the JE3 Foundation is now his full-time job, and as much as it is a comfort, it can sometimes be hard to relive his father's death in pursuit of the foundation's goals.

'There's times where it's too much,' he says. 'But also, around the corner, there's always something really good. Whether that's a life saved, whether that's us training 50 people that have never been taught the skill before.'

I ask Charlie about the famous line associated with Justin, 'I'm not here for the sake of it, I'm here for the fucking memories.' It was, according to Ross Embleton, originally his phrase. But whoever said it first, Justin made it famous.

'You can put that quote into any aspect of life you want to,' adds Charlie. 'And it's a quote I live by now. You don't know when your time's up. And I'm not here for the sake of it. I'm not just here to be a number and plod along. I'm here to achieve something. I'm here to make an impact. I'm here to leave a legacy. I'm here to make memories, not just for myself, but for other people. I think it's immensely powerful.'

Of course, it wasn't only Justin Edinburgh and Richie Wellens who made the memories happen. It was everyone else at Leyton Orient. From the fans, and staff, to the players and the management. And of course, the owners.

'I never set out to be involved in running Leyton Orient,' Nigel Travis tells me. 'And I am very proud. I've loved every minute.'

Nobody at Leyton Orient is there for the sake of it.

CHAPTER 19

1966 was a big year for English football

Nothing endures in football. Even names change. In 1966 Leyton Orient dropped the Leyton and became simply Orient. A successful fan-led campaign saw the club reinstate Leyton as part of the name in 1987, but it's rare for anything to stay the same in football. The club have played at Brisbane Road since 1937, the same ground with various improvements and tweaks – the home of Leyton Orient has been the same stadium for nearly a century. But even that will change. To grow, the club needs a bigger stadium, and the location of Brisbane Road, the surrounding terraced houses and flats embedded in the ground, mean a new site will need to be found.

Nothing endures.

Managers come and go all the time. Players just as much. Professional football is a transient game. It doesn't mean these people don't care about the club. They just have to move on. People get better offers or they don't get offered a new contract. We all know this.

We know that owners sell up and board members resign. Some fans decide something is more important in their life than football. They still check the scores, but maybe they don't go any more. You can sit near someone for a decade, and then one season they're just not there. They're skint, they got bored, they moved. They died. Who knows?

But Ada Martin endures. When I speak to him, he's been at Leyton Orient for over 30 years. It's people like Ada who make a football club more than just a name you read when you check the scores on your phone. People like Ada make it real. They make it last.

I ask him, how does it feel to be such a key part of Leyton Orient for over 30 years?

'It makes you proud,' he says. 'Like a badge of honour that I've stood around for that long. People always go back to the season with the Italians. I could have gone, but I didn't. If you're going to leave a club like this, one you've supported all your life, it would be on your terms, not on someone else's.

'I never thought I'd be here for this long. When you're young, you don't know what you're going to do in your life. And it always takes a different course. But working for a club who you've supported all your life; it's not really a job. There's only 92 of you in the country aren't there? Ninety-two football managers, 92 groundsmen, 92 kit managers. You're just lucky that you work somewhere where you like to work.'

This book has told the story of the past decade. But Ada, like many of the people I've spoken to, has been keen to talk about the future. There's a buzz around the Orient. Fans and staff have seen the good, they've seen the bad and they've seen the Becchetti. And now they see a bright future.

'For a club like Orient, looking up rather than down or sideways is massive,' continues Ada. 'It makes you want to be a part of it even more, because you want to be part of that next chapter. I honestly think we've got a chance to crack League One and to be a Championship side.'

That is the goal. In 2024, Nigel Travis and the board stated that they want to make Orient an established second-tier team. Sustainable, stable and fighting for their right to be heard among the 'Glory, Glory' of Tottenham Hotspur, the mystical 'West Ham Way' and the old money of Arsenal. Little Leyton Orient are growing. Travis's goal is for Orient to still be in existence in 100 years' time. But how big can they be?

'I think we can go that next step,' says Ada. 'You've just got to look at your Lutons and your Brentfords. It's not all pie-in-the-sky stuff. Maybe in ten years' time when I turn 60, I could be sitting here talking about your next book. And we're sitting here thinking, "We've got Man United first game of the season in the league." Why not?'

CHAPTER 19

Maybe, after the fall and the rise, this club is still rising.

Ultimately though, it doesn't matter. What matters is that Leyton Orient exists. The club, the fans, the staff, the players. They can dare to dream.

I will speak to Ada in ten years' time. Leyton Orient will still be here.

Acknowledgements

FOR A 'small' club, there's a lot of people who want to talk about Leyton Orient. I'm grateful to them all. I can't thank Paul Levy enough for being my first interviewee and explaining the project to Matt Porter. Matt, you have gone above and beyond. This book wouldn't be here without your support.

Everyone I spoke to at Leyton Orient was so generous with their time. Thank you to Kent Teague, Nigel Travis and Marshall Taylor for not only saving the club, but for being so accommodating with my requests. Barry Hearn, you made me feel so welcome when we spoke. And thank you for only asking for a copy of the book as payment. I think we can manage that.

Russell Slade, Martin Ling, Paul Terry, Ross Embleton, Jobi McAnuff, Dan Happe and Darren Pratley, thank you for your time and honesty. There's special thanks to Richie Wellens, not only for his time and honesty, but for being the only person who asked for a cut of the royalties. If I get any, you can have some.

Huge thanks to Dave Victor, Andy Gilson, Matt Simpson, Tom Davies, Howard Gould, Ada Martin, Barry Galvin and Steve Dixon. Your insights into this wonderful club were invaluable. Mark Hannah, Keren Harrison and Billy Herring, thank you for re-living both the glory days and the not so glory days with me.